NOTTINGHAM
& DERBYSHIRE
AIRFIELDS
IN THE SECOND
WORLD WAR

Robin J. Brooks

COUNTRYSIDE BOOKS
NEWBURY, BERKSHIRE

First published 2003
© Robin J. Brooks 2003
Reprinted 2007

COUNTRYSIDE BOOKS
3 Catherine Road
Newbury, Berkshire

To view our complete range of books,
please visit us at
www.countrysidebooks.co.uk

ISBN 978 1 85306 799 0

Designed by Mon Mohan
The cover painting is from an original by Colin Doggett and
shows Lancasters of No 1661 HCU lifting off from RAF Winthorpe.

Typeset by Textype, Cambridge
Produced through MRM Associates Ltd., Reading
Printed by Cambridge University Press

*All material for the manufacture of this book
was sourced from sustainable forests.*

CONTENTS

AREA MAP OF NOTTINGHAMSHIRE & DERBYSHIRE AIRFIELDS

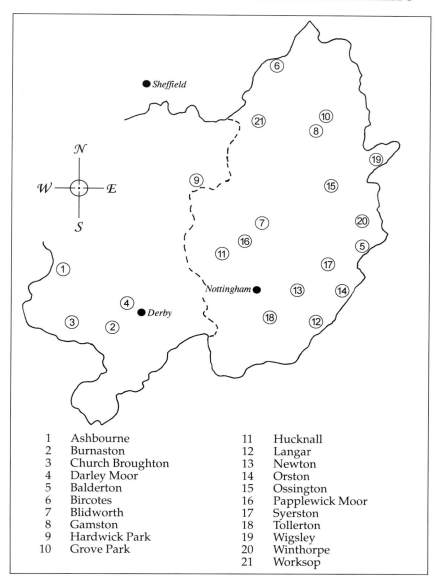

1	Ashbourne	11	Hucknall
2	Burnaston	12	Langar
3	Church Broughton	13	Newton
4	Darley Moor	14	Orston
5	Balderton	15	Ossington
6	Bircotes	16	Papplewick Moor
7	Blidworth	17	Syerston
8	Gamston	18	Tollerton
9	Hardwick Park	19	Wigsley
10	Grove Park	20	Winthorpe
		21	Worksop

INTRODUCTION

'Everything that I have worked for, everything that I have hoped for, everything that I believed in during my public life has crashed into ruins this morning. There is only one thing left for me and that is to devote what strength and powers I have to forwarding the victory of the cause for which we have to sacrifice ourselves. I cannot tell what part I may be allowed to play myself. I trust I may live to see the day when Hitlerism has been destroyed and a restored and liberated Europe has been re-established.'

So spoke a very sick Neville Chamberlain on 3rd September 1939. Over the coming months and the decisive period of 1940, far from the battle front of the south, most of the airfields in Nottinghamshire and Derbyshire were in the planning stage. The East Midlands came within the bounds of No 12 Group of Fighter Command, with its HQ at Watnall near Nottingham and whose fighter airfields therefore offered protection from enemy attacks to the Midlands and beyond. When the Nottinghamshire and Derbyshire airfields were eventually built and ready for use by 1941, those two counties became bomber counties. Although intended to house operational bomber squadrons, the majority became home to Operational Training Units. It was from these bases that young men, British and Polish, trained to become purveyors of bombs. Night and day saw them living with the dangers of flying in bad weather, of learning to navigate, of getting lost and facing technical problems with the aircraft, all of which caused many of them to perish in accidents.

The two counties were manufacturing areas where aero-engines and munitions were made. The giant Rolls-Royce plant in Derby were producing the magnificent Merlin engine that was to power so many aircraft and help the RAF win the Battle of Britain, and the munitions factories of Nottingham and Derby were producing ammunition for all kinds of guns. Whilst both cities were potential targets for the Luftwaffe and did suffer several raids, that they were not entirely obilterated was due to faulty German intelligence, out of date maps that their aircrews used and the bending of their navigational electronic aids or beams. For the latter we must thank a system developed in top secret by British scientists.

The civilians saw death and suffering at first hand in the raids on both counties. Many were to lose loved ones as the terror of bombing continued. Rallied on by the speeches of the charismatic Winston Churchill and the sense of camaraderie that war seemed to generate, they came through it all and victory was that much sweeter.

The airfields of Nottinghamshire and Derbyshire played their part in reaching that victory. I dedicate the following pages to all the military and civilian personnel who were killed, injured or suffered in any way from the results of greed and idealism.

Robin J. Brooks

Getting ready for a raid – No 408 (Goose) Squadron RCAF
(408 Sqdn via V. Baker)

I
SETTING THE SCENE

With the Battle of Britain over and won by the RAF, thoughts turned to how best to carry the war back to Germany. Bomber Command had formed in July 1936 and, although equipped with out-dated biplanes, plans were well advanced for these to be replaced by twin-engined, faster monoplanes. The Command itself had adopted a policy of bombing the enemy by night, forced on them by the fact that the Luftwaffe fighter force was far superior numerically. As the new monoplanes such as the Bristol Blenheim and the Wellington began to reach the squadrons, the demand for aircrew to man them became intense. The Blenheim carried a crew of three, but as aircraft became larger, so they demanded even further aircrew.

Thousands of young men from Britain and the Commonwealth came forward to be trained. Arriving at an Initial Training Wing, they would be taught the basic theory of flying, air force law, navigation, aircraft recognition and, of course, drill before being graded into different classifications of aircrew such as pilot, navigator, wireless operator/bomb aimer or gunner. For pilots, the introduction to flying would take place at an Elementary Flying Training School. In many cases, pupils were sent to one of the Dominions or the USA to learn to fly, such was the demand at this time. It must be recognised that the Commonwealth Air Training Plan (previously known as the Empire Air Training Plan), which incorporated countries such as Australia, Canada, South Africa, Rhodesia and New Zealand, trained over 75,000 pilots, 40,500 navigators, over 15,600 bomb aimers and nearly 38,000 air gunners. Without this help Bomber

Vickers Wellingtons of No 300 (Polish) Bomber Squadron (Crown)

Command could never have achieved the force it eventually became.

Once the elementary stage of training had been completed, pupil pilots were graded into single-engine and multi-engine training. In the two counties covered in this book, it was the multi-engined aircraft which entailed further flying training at a Service Flying Training School operating twin-engined Airspeed Oxfords or Avro Ansons. Once the trainees had gained their wings, usually after a total of 130 hours' flying instruction, they would move on to an Operational Training Unit (OTU) to fly aircraft such as Battles, Whitleys, Wellingtons and Hampdens, as well as the aforementioned Ansons and Blenheims. Most of these aircraft had been the mainstay of Bomber Command during the opening phases of the war, but by 1942, as the larger, four-engined aircraft such as the Stirling, Lancaster and Halifax came onstream, they had been relegated to training duties. Now the pilots would be flying these aircraft all over the UK in all weathers, taking part in 'nickelling' (leaflet dropping) raids over Channel ports as a prelude to operational bombing.

At the OTU the men would be invited to 'crew up' as all the differently trained aircrew came together at last. There was no

The Avro Anson was used in a taxi role by the ATA. This is a later model, C.19. (MAP)

Handley Page Hampdens of No 14 OTU. This type was the workhorse of many of the East Midlands units. (IWM)

military pattern for this selection, it came together naturally as each person got to know another by just talking and mixing. Once a crew was made up, it stayed together for the course. Once the members had 'gelled', an intense course of operational flying training began, which for some would end in tragedy as aircraft systems failed and crews became lost in the appalling English weather. Those that did survive were posted to a Heavy Conversion Unit to begin flying on operations.

The crews would then be flying the large, four-engined bombers mentioned above, and included in this category must be the Avro Manchester. Although still twin-engined, the RAF had high hopes for the type, with its range and bomb load and the added bonus of being simple to build and maintain. Its one failure was its two Rolls-Royce Vulture engines, which proved to be under-powered and unreliable. From the design, however, came the Lancaster fitted with four Rolls-Royce Merlin engines. It was this aircraft that was to carry much of the war back to Germany.

The captain and crew of a Lancaster OTU – left to right: navigator, radio op, rear gunner, captain, co-pilot. (Crown)

Derbyshire and Nottinghamshire were bomber, OTU and training territory. The former had just five airfields: Ashbourne and its satellite at Darley Moor, together with Burnaston, which also trained army pilots to fly gliders, Hardwick Park and Church Broughton. What the county did have was a proliferation of heavy manufacturing industry all contributing to the war effort. Notable among these was Rolls-Royce, designer and builder of many aero-engines, the most famous being the Merlin. It was this engine that powered the Defiant, Hurricane and Spitfire fighters and the Battle, Lancaster, Mosquito and Whitley bombers, together with various Fleet Air Arm aircraft of the period.

Nottinghamshire, on the other hand, whilst also the home of heavy industry, had OTUs and bomber stations. And it had Poles! Those brave countrymen whose hatred of the common enemy was exceeded by no-one. The county was to host four Polish bomber squadrons as well as a number of Polish training units. What they lacked in knowledge of the English language they made up for in sheer 'guts'. Many of them fell in the service of this country as the Polish war graves in the Newark on Trent cemetery indicate. Their impact on the county remains today for there is a strong Polish element living happily within the area.

Of the bomber stations, Balderton was one of the largest. Opened in 1941, it began life as an OTU before becoming home to a Canadian bomber squadron. It was further used by a glider maintenance unit and a Heavy Conversion Unit before being handed over to the USAAF to accommodate a Troop Carrier Group tasked with taking part in Operation 'Market', the airborne element of Operation 'Market Garden', the drop at Arnhem. Reverting back to RAF control, it housed a Lancaster squadron before closing in 1945 and eventually being destroyed during the construction of the A1 Newark bypass.

Langar was also used extensively by bombers, with part of the airfield incorporating an Aircraft Repair Unit belonging to A V Roe Ltd. Langar was also handed over to the USAAF for a Troop Carrier Group, again in connection with the Arnhem operation. When they left, in 1946, Langar closed, but was re-activated by the Royal Canadian Air Force, who used the site for eleven years as an air material base. When they left, Langar also saw the closure of the A V Roe Ltd complex and was left under Care and Maintenance. It continued this way for many years

Polish airmen at an English lesson. (Crown)

A Whitley tows a Horsa glider in a practice for D Day. (IWM CH10343)

until sold by the military, when it became the home of a branch of the British Parachute Schools. Though on a limited scale, Langar is once again a flying and living airfield.

It was to Syerston that Guy Gibson came before he found fame as the leader of the Dams raid. A flight commander with No 106 Squadron, he carried out many bombing raids flying from the airfield before he was posted elsewhere. Flt Lt 'Bill' Reid was to gain a Victoria Cross with No 61 Squadron whilst at Syerston. His citation stated 'that he showed a tenacity and devotion to duty beyond praise' when, badly wounded, he managed to get his crew home safely when his Lancaster was barely airworthy.

Various units continued to use the airfield throughout the war until, like most of the others, it closed in the late 1970s. The two remaining bomber stations in Nottinghamshire were Wigsley and Winthorpe. Both contributed to the strength of Bomber Command and today Winthorpe is the home of the greatly acclaimed Newark Air Museum.

The remaining airfields were used in the training role. Bircotes, Gamston, Newton, Ossington, Tollerton and Worksop, plus several minor airfields, all contributed so much to the supply of aircrew for Bomber Command. When Arthur 'Bomber' Harris became the C-in-C of the command on 23rd February 1942, morale leapt to a new height. His '1,000 bomber' raids resulted in Albert Speer, Hitler's armaments minister, later stating that the bomber war was 'the greatest battle we lost'. Today it is easy for the modern media to reflect on and, in most cases, condemn the morality of saturation bombing. Most of them were not around at this time of war. Bomber Command's success, however, was not achieved without an immense loss of life: 55,573 men lost their lives and many thousands were injured. It was a colossal price to pay.

For that, the airfields of the two counties contributed greatly to the final victory. Though no operational airfields now exist, what they helped achieve in wartime should never be forgotten; the memory will always be cherished.

2
PREPARATIONS FOR WAR

Airfield Construction

Formation and composition of construction groups

In 1934 there were 52 RAF airfields in the UK, most of which had been constructed by civilian labour. A think-tank some years later estimated that 700 would need to be ready by 1942. Before 1939 it was the responsibility of the army, ie the Royal Engineers, to oversee the construction of most airfields. With war, pressure of work for the engineers forced the Air Ministry to think of forming its own airfield construction units. Several Air Ministry Works Directorates officers were selected and instructed to form units consisting of civil engineers, surveyors and mechanical and electrical engineers. On 15 March 1940, the first unit was ready.

Later in 1940, the Battle of Britain brought heavy bombing attacks on the south east airfields and it was sections of the Royal Engineers that were called upon to repair the bomb damage. The War Office, however, informed the Air Ministry that this could Not continue due to the engineer units being needed for military duties and training in combat. The Air Ministry decided once more to form its own units, this time to be called 'works squadrons', each one having a headquarters and ten 'works flights'. Each flight was to consist of a few qualified tradesmen supported by unskilled personnel.

The Airfield Construction Service, as it was known, came under the control of W10 (ACS), a branch of the Air Ministry Works Directorate. Again, lack of manpower became a problem because so many men were on active service. In mid-1941, the Ministry of Labour had allocated the Air Ministry 97,000 men. This was in reply to a warning from the Secretary of State for Air, Sir Archibald Sinclair, to the effect that unless the Air Ministry was given more manpower, the rate of building would not keep up with the expected damage from an increase in enemy air attacks. This was to prove the case in the North Midland Region (NMR), which covered both Nottinghamshire and Derbyshire and was where many of the new airfields were being built. Out of the area's total labour force of 58,500 in October 1941, 37,600 of the civilian labour force were engaged upon airfield construction. By January 1942, this had been reduced by 4,300, partly to meet the needs of the Ministry of Aircraft Production, which were considered a priority. In March of the same year, the Secretary of State for Air told the Ministry of Labour that unless 15,000 to 20,000 men were transferred into the NMR and the Eastern Region (ER), the airfield building programme would be set back two to three months at least. Bearing this in mind, the cabinet decided to delay the call-up of 15,000 available men and keep them on the building programme. Over the same period, the USAAF, realising the manpower situation on airfield construction, approached Washington to allow American engineers and builders to come to the UK to assist. The result was that twenty-four US Army Engineer Aviation Battalions arrived to push the programme along.

The Expansion Period

An important aspect of the growth of airfields was the Expansion Period. Practically all the existing airfields in the UK that were earmarked for expansion had been constructed during the First World War. They had received very little maintenance during the inter-war period and so required much attention. In November 1933, a committee was set up to 'examine deficiencies in national and imperial defence'. One year later, the Commander-in-Chief of Air Defence of Great Britain (ADGB), Air Chief Marshal Sir

Robert Brooke-Popham, devised the 're-orientation scheme', which gave the period a kick start. Under the new scheme, the ADGB was scrapped in July 1936 to be replaced by four commands – fighter, bomber, coastal and training – each requiring its own design of airfield. The overall bias was towards bomber airfields, which would be needed to carry the war back to the enemy when required. A scheme known as Scheme 'L' was put into operation. This was the latest alphabetical scheme, its predecessors being coded from 'A' to the final 'L' and carrying varying ideas and projections.

In order to meet the requirements of the scheme, the Air Ministry Aerodromes Board was formed within the Air Ministry Works Directorate and headed by Air Vice Marshal C A H Longcroft, CB, DSO, AFC and Air Commodore J D Boyle CBE, DSO. The Board worked closely with the Air Ministry Lands branch, whose duties were to handle the legal side of land acquisition. To be eligible, sites had to be five miles apart, free from obstructions, such as buildings and trees, and above sea level, but by no more than 600 feet, thus reducing the risk of low cloud and fog. Good drainage was also a requirement. When such areas were found, it was just a case of walking across them and evaluating any apparent dangers.

Such was the urgency and speed at which the Board worked that from 1935 to the beginning of war one hundred new airfields were built and a large upgrading programme carried out on existing ones. As we will read in the chapters on individual airfields, only three in Nottinghamshire and Derbyshire had their origins pre-war, those being Burnaston, Newton and Papplewick Moor. The rest were hastily built during the 1939/41 period.

When war did eventually come, many small airfields and local flying clubs were requisitioned by the military. In addition to the three airfields mentioned, it is recorded that Alan Cobham brought his National Aviation Days Tour to both Derby and Nottingham on several occasions and could have used any of the airfields.

During the Expansion Period, it had been decided that the airfields already built and those under planning in the area known as middle England should be for bomber and training purposes. A standard pattern was devised for all the sites, including the designs of buildings. Even at this time of tension, the designs of the pre-war permanent airfield buildings had to conform to a set standard and had to meet the demands of the Royal Fine Arts Commission and the Society for the Preservation of Rural England. The buildings that are today still standing on some of the old wartime airfields, and the ones that are still operational, give credence to the fact that they were very well built.

The Air Ministry Directorate-General of Works standard for bomber stations, OTUs etc was designated a Class 'A' Type airfield. This included enlarged original stations as well as new. Three intersecting runways were essential, the main one equipped with some form of lighting. Aligned with the prevailing wind, most were initially grass, but as aircraft got larger and heavier the soft surface was inadequate; by 1943 many had a main runway of tarmac or concrete. With this addition the cost of building naturally spiralled. In 1939 the cost of building a bomber airfield was set at £550,000. By 1945 it had risen to

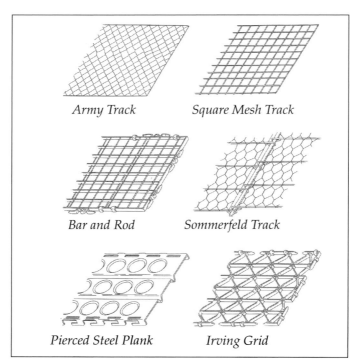

Army Track   Square Mesh Track

Bar and Rod   Sommerfeld Track

Pierced Steel Plank   Irving Grid

(Chris Samson)

£1,000,000. Consider the cost today of upgrading or building a new airfield.

Many of the well known civilian companies were involved in building during the Expansion Period (1936–45): John Laing, George Wimpey, Richard Costain, Sir Alfred McAlpine and many others. The building of the airfields was the biggest engineering feat since the railways in the 19th century. That many of them are still in use today is a testimony to their construction.

In considering the main airfields, we must not forget that most of them had either a satellite, a relief landing ground or an emergency landing ground. Satellites had hard runways, while RLGs and ELGs were grass. The Chester seed firm of James Hunter Ltd were consulted frequently as to what type of grass to sow when it came to problems with drainage and durability. During the course of the war, some grass airfields did acquire a hard runway and some were fitted with Sommerfeld Tracking or similar to ensure better serviceability. The main types used are illustrated (*see opposite page*).

As the airfields were being constructed, other personnel arrived to put up the buildings. The designs were numerous but the main ones, again, have stood the test of time. The Airfield Construction Squadrons that covered the East Midlands were Nos. 5001, 5002, 5003 and 5004.

Airfield Buildings

Hangars

From the Expansion Period to modern day, there have been many hangar designs. Before 1935, the more usual type to be seen was the 'A' Type, which had a span of 120 feet and a length of 250 feet. Another that was in common use around the same period was the Belfast Truss Hangar, fine examples of which can be seen at Hucknall airfield in Nottinghamshire. As aircraft got larger so the need for a bigger hangar became prevalent and the 'C' Type, created by the design branch of the Directorate General of Works, came about. It had sliding doors at each end, a span of 150 feet and was 300 feet in length. Examples of this hangar can be seen at many airfields today. Trees were planted alongside the hangars, together with a further clever camouflage system. Rooms were built along the length of the hangar for stores, squadron offices etc, with the recently closed RAF airfield at Newton near Nottingham having five very good examples of this hangar. Being large, the building of such hangars was very time consuming, so simpler utility versions were built. Of far quicker construction was the Bellman Hangar. Somewhat smaller, it was an all-welded shed with a door height of 25 feet. Covered in corrugated steel sheeting, from 1938 to 1939 over 400 were constructed. It was, however, the steel firm of Sir William Arrol and Co Ltd that in 1939 came up with a design that, whilst having similar dimensions to the 'C' Type, was far easier and quicker to assemble. Known as the 'J' and 'K' Types, they were of metal construction with curved roofs of steel plate. The 'J' was intended for operational stations whilst the 'K' was intended for aircraft storage.

Regarding the storage of aircraft, it was in 1936 that a start was made on hangars for Aircraft Storage Units (ASUs). These were normally placed in dispersal sites around the airfields, but could be built on any flat area adjacent to the main site. These hangars came under three main classifications and were known as 'D', 'L'

'C' type hangars on a rainy day in 2002. (Author)

22

and 'E' Type hangars. The 'D' was constructed of concrete, had a curving roof and was again the creation of the Directorate General of Works design team. It had vertical side walls whereas the 'E' and 'L' had a roof that curved directly from the ground. Time dictated the need for further and larger hangars and, after some deliberation, the Air Ministry, in collaboration with the Tees-side Bridge and Engineering Works, produced a hangar classified as the 'T' Type. It was produced in three sizes: the Tl had a 95-foot span, the T2 a 115-foot span and the T3 a 66-foot span. This eventually became one of the most common types to be seen at airfields and by 1945, over 900 had been erected on airfields all over the country.

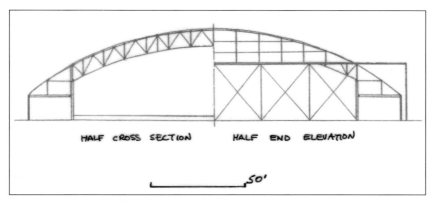

A 'K' type hangar (Chris Samson)

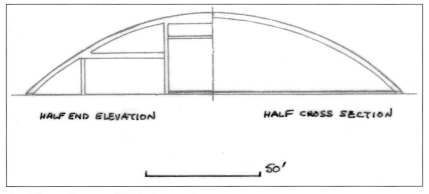

An 'E' type hangar (Chris Samson)

There were several other minor designs of hangar, but it was the Bellman and 'T' Types that were the most prevalent, many of which are still standing today. Despite this, surely the hangar that evokes the most nostalgia has to be the Blister Hangar. Sited mainly around dispersal areas, the Blister was produced by Messrs C Miskins and Sons in 1939. With a prototype built at Biggin Hill in Kent during January 1940, three types were eventually put into production. Easy and quick to construct, they were of wooden arched rib construction clad with corrugated steel sheeting and a facility to put curtains up at each end. Whilst the latter may appear odd, on wet and windy airfields, especially dispersal areas, any protection from the elements was gratefully received. Some airmen even went so far as to brick up one end of the hangar, therefore eliminating any draught whatsoever. The three types supplied were the Standard Blister with a span of 45 feet, the Over Blister having a 65-foot span and the Extra Over Blister with a span of 69 feet. All three were 45 feet long. Over 3,000 of the type were supplied to the RAF and many are still in use today, not so much on airfields but for agricultural purposes, having been dismantled at their previous sites and resurrected on farm land. Very few new hangars have been built today for the old have stood the test of time. The hangars built post 1970s are more likely to be Hardened Aircraft Shelters which were to be used for dispersal and protection during the Cold War.

Camouflage

As early as 1935 the Director of Works had pointed out to the Air Staff the need for good camouflage on the airfields. Protecting them against air attack was a growing concern throughout the Expansion Period but at that time the advice was not heeded and when war came in 1939 there was a rush to develop several ways in which to camouflage the buildings. The hangars mentioned previously were camouflaged from the onset of war, but any erected after 1942 were finished in black bitumen, often covered in camouflage nets. Natural camouflage came in the shape of trees and hedges. Although this formed part of the overall camouflage plans, it was not until 1939 that the thought was taken very seriously. A noted artist of the time, Norman Wilkinson, was given the honorary rank of Air Commodore and told to form a section to take on the task of camouflage.

Experimental work had been carried out at Cranwell before the war when buildings were painted brown and green to enable them to blend in with the surrounding countryside. Landing areas were marked by black bitumen laid on the grass, to give the impression of a field by field landscape and not a large area of grass. When the hardened perimeter tracks and hardstandings were built, a problem became evident whenever it rained: they shone. In order to alleviate this, experiments were carried out using slag chippings. In Nottinghamshire, the bomber stations with hard runways were initially treated to an overlay of hard chippings. These, however, caused many aircraft tyres to burst. Several other materials were experimented with, including sawdust and seaweed, but in the end the only really successful method was wood chips. This method eventually became standard when, with the war being carried back to the enemy, camouflage was not so important.

Mention must be made of the camouflage system deployed at the Nightingale Road factory of Rolls-Royce. In order to blot out the obvious features of the workshops, ie long stretches of glass panes in the roof covering a vast area, wooden screens were placed over much of the glass. In addition, the roofs were painted in various colours and different shapes in order to give the impression of houses and gardens. Along the front of the building various designs had also been painted to resemble a row of houses. That it worked can be gauged by the very few raids that Rolls-Royce suffered, although there were several other factors involved. Much of the original wartime camouflage can be seen on the hangars and buildings in use today.

Decoy Airfields

According to the records, three airfields in Nottinghamshire had decoy airfields. They were all 'Q', or night-time sites, and were decoys for Newton (Cotgrave and Tithby), Ossington (Upton) and Syerston (Kneeton). Other decoy sites were built to protect the cities, and it is right that the reader is informed about the effort and time put into such a project.

The First World War had demonstrated the value of decoys, but after the armistice nothing further was done until 1932.

During that year the Air Ministry did hold talks regarding the future of the decoy matter but the idea was then shelved until 1938. It fell to Alexander Korda of London Films to approach the Ministry with the offer of the use of his studio and staff at Denham. It was suggested that they might be embodied into a part-time air defence unit, and whilst this was quashed before it got off the ground it did sow the seed of an idea that their work of deception and 'make-believe' in films could be used to deceive the enemy. With the war only two weeks old, a meeting at Bomber Command Headquarters was convened to discuss the subject. In the end it was decided that two types of decoy site should be constructed. One was known as the 'K' site, which would counter day attacks and have dummy aircraft and buildings, and the other was a 'Q' site, which would have airfield lighting etc for night attacks. It was finally decided to approach the British film industry to provide the expertise and Shepperton Studios in Middlesex was chosen. Within the studios was a company called Sound City, which had experience in making sets for filming. The man placed in charge was Colonel Sir John Fisher Turner, a First World War Royal Engineers officer, and for the sake of security the department became known as Colonel Turner's Department.

The first job was to find suitable sites fairly close to the parent airfield. Once they were selected, the legal formalities began with the local landowners whose land was to be requisitioned. Once this was done, work began on cutting down bushes, filling in holes and laying out two dummy runways. Negotiations were on-going with several film studios including Warner Brothers and Gaumont British Studios for the assembly of decoy aircraft. With the realisation that the enemy would attempt to bomb the country into submission, an air of urgency became apparent; so much so that by January 1940, the first 'K' and 'Q' sites were operational. By 1st August, whilst the Battle of Britain was raging down south, thirty-six 'K' and fifty-six 'Q' sites were in use. The dummy aircraft placed on the 'K' sites were various. Hurricanes, Blenheims, Battles and even Wellingtons were all constructed of wood, cardboard and any other cheap materials available. When a canvas was stretched over the framework, the appearance from the air was remarkably lifelike. Some work was carried out by civilian companies engaged in furniture production and similar crafts, for as the war progressed the Shepperton Studios were hard pressed to complete all the work. Later dummies were constructed of a metal tube frame covered with a rubber canvas and, even later, inflatable aircraft were produced. By 1942, with the decline in mass daylight bombing, most of the 'K' sites had closed leaving only three operational. The 'Q' sites were to carry on for longer.

Most of the 'Q' sites had become operational by mid-1940. Some were set up near or next to 'K' sites, thus in effect becoming 'KQ' sites. With the object of encouraging the enemy to bomb these sites, runway lights were essential to their success. Initially Goose-neck flares were used but these proved time consuming so Glim Electric Lights were tried next powered by one or two generators housed in control bunkers just below ground level. These were even later replaced by the Drem runway lighting system, which included outer perimeter and totem pole lighting. With the increased success of the night-fighter squadrons in shooting down enemy raiders, and the fact that large bomber formations were fast diminishing, the need for the 'Q' sites also rapidly diminished and by 1943 most had been shut down.

Another decoy worthy of mention is the 'Starfish' sites. From 1941 onwards, the towns and cities of the UK came under increasing night-time attacks. It was observed that most of the enemy bombers conformed to a 'follow the leader' pattern and dropped their bombs on the fire that was forthcoming from the initial drop. It was also known that the enemy had electronic navigation technology known as 'Knickebein', a system using two radio beams broadcast from ground stations across the Channel to intercept over the chosen target. In order to combat this new technology, the RAF formed No 80 (Signals) Wing, who became competent at 'bending' or 'jamming' the beams, thus rendering the enemy's navigation faulty, enticing them to drop their bombs at the first sign of fire below.

Thoughts thus turned to a way of lighting large fires away from the towns and cities in order to save the main targets. Known initially as 'special fires', they were eventually called 'Starfish' sites. Some places had one site, others had two, three and so on. A few of the larger cities had the fires lit all around them, plus a system of lighting that could be colour changed to give the impression of street lighting or building lighting. These sites became known as 'Starfish/QL' and were complete with generators and semi-underground bunkers for the personnel to

A mobile dummy Spitfire (above) and a dummy Mustang (below). These are two of many erected to deceive the enemy. (PRO Air 20/4349)

control them from. It fell mainly to airmen to man the sites, though, later, some came under the control of the army. It is interesting to note that the 'Starfish' sites were built and in use in the Midlands by November 1940, including several for our two counties. Records tell us that Starfish sites for the city of Nottingham were situated at Cropwell Butler, Clipston, Barton in Fabis and Lowdham, whilst the Derby sites were at Ticknall, Diseworth and Swarkestone. There is no doubt that they deflected many raids from the city centres, but by 1944, as the Allies closed on Berlin, most sites had closed.

The statistics of the decoy programme were considerable and the cost ran into millions of pounds. A dummy Wellington would cost £400 to build, Blenheims and Whitleys around £150 and a Battle £90. Despite this, the programme certainly saved many airfields, towns and cities from total destruction and therefore saved many military and civilian lives. The phantom Air Force and fire deception had played its part well.

Control Towers

They stand like sentinels on many of the old wartime airfields. The Watch Office or, as it is now termed, Control Tower, is usually the last building to survive the ravages of time. Many wartime ones are still in use today, albeit with a modern glass observation tower fitted to the top. Prior to the outbreak of war, airfield control was non-existent. Pilots were advised to keep a sharp look-out when preparing to land or depart and the only regulation was that they signed in and out of the Duty Pilot's log-book. All of this, of course, had to change when war came and the Watch Office became an important building on the airfield.

The tower usually consisted of a single storey building with windows at the front and both sides. Designed by the Air Ministry and known as a 518/40 Type Watch Office, it was adequate for the opening phases of the war. As the tempo increased, larger premises were required. One way to achieve this without too much expense and trouble was to add an extra storey to the original building. Only a few of this type remain standing today.

As the airfield building programme continued during 1941/42, it was decided to upgrade the Watch Office to a proper tower. The 12779/41 Type was the next development – a two storey building with a roof access for better observation. Windows were again in the front and the two sides. Another two storey version with the designation 518/40 was a tower with an additional look-out tower built at the back end. There were several other designs which, as the war progressed, came into use, but they were variations of the 1277/41 Type tower. Two of the best remaining Control Towers in the county of Nottinghamshire are at Langar and Newton. Usually sited alongside the perimeter track for all-round observation, the Control Towers also had a signals square directly in front of the building. Outlined in white concrete, it gave indications of the runway in use, direction of circuit and an identifying letter for the airfield. Post-war, many of the wartime towers were adapted with the addition of a local control room with greater window area on top of the original brick.

Many of the old towers left standing are in a state of decay and are supposedly haunted by the airmen who used them. Fact or

The post-war control tower at RAF Newton seen in 2002. (Author)

fiction? No-one really knows, but the eerie feeling that one gets when entering is certainly fact.

Accommodation and Technical

There are many types of hutted, concrete and asbestos buildings surviving on many of the airfields. Development of domestic and technical buildings accelerated from the Expansion Period up until the cessation of war. As we have already read, consultation for certain brick buildings on permanent stations such as Newton had to be agreed between the main conservation bodies of the period. Thus, many buildings such as the Officers' Mess were based on a neo-Georgian design. The NCOs', Sergeants' and airmen's messes were similarly designed and built. The technical buildings were also of standard design, yet huts seemed to be of various shapes and sizes. One of the first was the 'B' Type hut, followed by the 'A' Type. The former was supposedly good for five years, the second for from ten to fifteen years, being built of

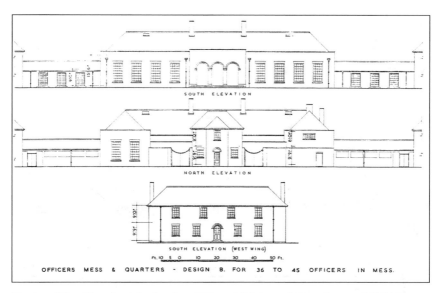

Design 'B' – Standard design for Officers' Mess and Quarters, c. 1939/44. (Author)

better materials. These were standard Air Ministry huts made of timber. However, with the demands of war, timber became scarce and alternative types were looked at which needed less timber or none at all. Several types were built including the Ministry of Supply timber hut, the Thorne hut, the Laing hut, made of light timber, plaster board and felt, and the Maycrete, made of pre-cast concrete blocks.

One particular hut, however, is the epitome of the wartime airfield building. Designed by Colonel P Nissen, it was in use during the First World War and was revived for the second conflict. The Nissen hut was used for accommodation, technical purposes, storage and practically everything else. Built in spans of 16, 24 and 30 feet, it had a concrete floor and steel ribs covered with corrugated steel sheeting, much like the domestic Anderson shelter. The Nissen hut too has stood the test of time with many still in use today.

There were several other types worthy of mention. The Handcraft hut was built with an asbestos curved roof and used mainly for storage; the Nashcrete hut was timber fronted and, again, had an asbestos roof. These and all of the other buildings are part of the nostalgia of the wartime airfields.

Defences

That there was a total lack of airfield defence was suddenly realised with the swift progress of the Germans across France. With their arrival at the French Channel ports, plans were hastily gathered to defend the airfields should the enemy attempt either an airborne or landborne invasion. Suddenly there was an urgency to dig trenches, construct shelters and find any type of anti-aircraft gun that was available. Spurred on by the words of Winston Churchill: 'Every man in RAF uniform ought to be armed with something, a rifle, a tommy gun, a pistol, a pike or a mace', by the end of 1940 the supply of guns and ammunition had improved considerably.

It fell to the army to be the first military to defend the airfields. The standard armour used comprised the Bofors gun, Lewis gun and various smaller calibres of gun. At various positions around the airfield, they were sited in gun pits or trenches. By 1941, the defence of airfields had been placed on a more thorough footing and a defence plan had been agreed to classify airfields. A Class I airfield was to have brick pillboxes around the perimeter with more to cover the dispersal areas. A Class 2 would have pillboxes, though on a reduced scale, whilst a Class 3 would have only one or two. One of the more interesting pillboxes, the Pickett-Hamilton Fort, would be placed on many of the major airfields, and although in principle a good idea, in practice it proved useless. Built over 60 years ago, pillboxes are still around today and are a constant reminder of the period. Some counties have even listed them as of architectural and historical interest and are determined to preserve them for future generations to see.

For many years the metal hatches seen buried in the grass at many airfields all over the country were assumed to be drains or soakaways for the surrounding large areas of grass. These hatches were, in fact, entrances to the Pickett/Hamilton Forts, more commonly known as retractable gun turrets. With a flight of three or four metal steps, the inside of the forts revealed a mass of mechanism and a compressed air bottle. This pillbox had its origins deep in the Weald of Kent for it was here at a farm near Tenterden that its inventor lived for many years. Francis Norman Pickett, engineer, financier and inventor, was the man behind many other wartime ideas, but it is mainly for the fort that he will be remembered.

Officially known as the Pickett/Hamilton Fort (the word Hamilton referring to pressure) they were placed on the majority of airfields, usually in groups of three, in late 1940. Lying alongside the main runway, they were not installed in time for the Battle of Britain but were thought to be effective for the on-going war. Manned by three gunners, the object of the fort was to pop up out of the ground and surprise enemy paratroopers when and if they invaded. At the conclusion of any action, the fort would sink back into the grass with the occupants still inside ready to do battle with the next wave.

There were two main designs for the retractable fort. The earlier design, dating from around 1938/39, was the Counter Balance Fort. Its operation required a detachment of at least three men, who entered the chamber via a steel trapdoor in the roof. The raising of the head was achieved by the men pushing up on the roof, a counterweight then taking over and raising the firing slits or platform above ground level. The action of the pillbox

The Pickett/Hamilton Fort showing the raised entry hatch. (Author)

was very quick, raising taking less than five seconds and lowering taking ten to twelve seconds.

This design was, however, improved upon and later models had a pneumatic mechanism. The inner section of the fort was raised by a ramrod device, originally operated by compressed air. The use of air, however, was found to be unreliable and so this was eventually replaced by oil hydraulic action carried out by one of the occupants using a pumping handle. Famous racing driver Donald Campbell was a friend of the inventor and he allowed his racing workshops to build the prototypes and himself took part in the original trials of the fort. In the second volume of his war history, Winston Churchill recorded a minute on the Pickett/Hamilton Fort. Sending it to General Ismay on 12 July 1941, he said: 'I saw these Pillboxes for the first time when I visited Langley last week. This appears to afford an admirable means of anti-parachute defence and it should surely be widely adopted. Let me have a plan.'

A total of 335 were installed at various airfields but due to the fact that the enemy never reached the UK, were never used in anger. Exercises with them, however, had already proved the device impractical, mainly due to flooding and difficulties in raising and lowering, plus the vulnerability of the men inside.

Another imaginative airfield defence system was the Parachute and Cable, though records show that this was only used on southern airfields. Worthy of mention, though, it consisted of a line of rockets to which were attached light steel cables carrying a parachute. Fired into the air as enemy aircraft approached the airfield they rose to around 600 feet, whereupon the parachutes would open automatically allowing the cable to descend slowly and, hopefully, ensnare the enemy aircraft whilst doing so. This method had limited success but, again, was a really good idea in principle.

In considering defences we must not forget the barrage balloon. The controlling command was formed in 1938 but it was not until a year later that serious consideration was given to the deployment of balloons. They were manned in the main by members of the auxiliary air force, and in September 1939 it

A familiar sight over the industrial Midlands – the Balloon Barrage. (SE Newspapers)

became necessary to form a second commanding group. It had been envisaged that 1,450 balloons would be deployed but the initial number fell far short of this. With the headquarters of Balloon Command being established at Stanmore under the command of Air Vice-Marshal O T Boyd, July 1940 saw the total of 'gas bags' rise to 1,400. The main task of the barrage was to keep the enemy aircraft at heights from which their bombing would be less accurate. Flown at varying heights, the maximum altitude was 5,000 feet, enough to deter even the most hardened enemy pilot. As the war progressed, many balloons were lost due to the enemy shooting them down, but also the weather could tear the balloon from its anchor cable. Sadly, many British aircraft also fell foul of the cables but the sight of a barrage over a key military site or a city was a reassuring sight to the populace.

In Derby, thirty sites were set up at strategic points, all controlled by No 918 (Balloon Barrage) Squadron. In addition to airmen, WAAFs were also beginning to man the sites, several around Derby being totally WAAF controlled. During the early months of the Phoney War, the balloon crews, like all watchers on the front line, needed a lot of patience. Some of the sites were situated near houses or huts that were requisitioned to become living quarters. In scorching sun, autumn gales and winter snow, they waited for the attack which they knew would eventually come. As we will read in the chapter on the bombing of Rolls-Royce, it was a balloon that very nearly brought down the one raider that damaged the factory. Together with the anti-aircraft gun barrage and the searchlights, the balloon earned its place in the history of defence.

In November 1941, it was recommended that the air force should have its own defence force. Accordingly, the RAF Regiment was formed on 1 February 1942, eventually taking the duty of airfield defence away from the army. From this time, a far stronger defence force evolved, equipped with modern weapons of the time. This new approach needed a co-ordinated pattern and in order to achieve this the Battle Headquarters came into existence on many major airfields. Known as the 11008/41 design, it was a reinforced concrete structure built to withstand any bomb attack. Sited on the highest point of the airfield and close to trees and hedges for concealment, the headquarters was dominated by a 6-foot square observation tower, 3 feet of which was semi-sunk into the ground. Incorporated in the top was a slit giving a 360 degree view of the airfield. Entrance was via a stairway at one end, which gave access to the sunken part containing a control room, sleeping accommodation and toilet. Many of the Battle Headquarters survive today due to the concrete structure but, unfortunately, many are flooded and therefore dangerous to enter.

The final method of airfield defence was the laying of pipe mines. If invasion had come then it would have been appropriate to deny the enemy the use of our airfields. The most common method was the Canadian Pipe Mine System. It consisted of a series of steel pipes packed with explosive which were laid beneath the surface at varying intervals, usually beside the runway or landing area. When detonated by hand, they would blow a crater measuring 12 to 15 feet wide and 4 to 5 feet deep. Whilst most of these mines were recovered after the war, some are still buried and active. Recently pipe mines were discovered and detonated at Detling airfield in Kent. (See *Kent Airfields in the Second World War*.)

Flying Training

E&RFTS

As we will read in the chapters detailing the airfields, the Elementary and Reserve Flying Training Schools were formed pre-war to train civilians to fly in order to provide the trained pilots whom the RAF would require in wartime. The schools were initially civilian-manned, receiving a contract from the Air Ministry, as was the case at Burnaston in Derbyshire where Air Schools Ltd ran No 30 E&RFTS. Would-be pilots had to be educated to School Certificate standard and between the ages of 18 and 25. By 1938, the E&RFTSs had become fully under Air Ministry control and were commanded by a regular officer.

EFTS

At the outbreak of war, the existing network of E&RFTS was re-organised and many schools closed. Some amalgamated to form Elementary Flying Training Schools and continued throughout the war in much the same way as the E&RFTS. Having completed the training, pupils moved on to Service Flying Training Schools.

Two students prepare for a flying lesson at Burnaston in 1939.
(Derby Library)

Civil Air Guard

In 1939, a question was asked in the House of Commons concerning the utility of the Civil Air Guard. Swiftly, the answer came that since its inception the CAG had made remarkable progress. Starting with little or no advance preparation, it had quickly settled down to a serious training programme and during the first four months of 1939 a total of 1,060 pupils had qualified for their 'A' licences.

The CAG scheme was launched in July 1938 by the Air Minister, Sir Kingsley Wood. Many civilian airfields and flying clubs registered for the scheme and there was no shortage of keen applicants. The provision of aircraft became one of the greatest difficulties. With the main manufacturers committed to military contracts, a well-known manufacturer of light aircraft proposed hiring them to the CAG, with the basic charge being subsidised by the Government.

The scheme was open to both sexes, though the majority of applicants were male. As well as flying, training students were asked to study navigation, airfield lighting and aviation law. The question of parachutes for CAG pupils was raised on more than one occasion. Previously refused due to the low altitude at which the pupils were taught to fly, a new classification for advanced training which allowed flying training to take place at higher altitudes did justify the use of parachutes.

The CAG ensured a ready supply of pilots for both the air force and the navy, yet when war came, it was felt by some that the RAF looked down upon pilots trained by the CAG. The new thinking was that they only wanted pilots trained by the RAF schools. Thus, many who had been in the CAG were disillusioned with the entire system. However, many people were able to obtain a pilot's licence, which, even if not used in anger, was certainly used in peacetime.

And so the scene was set for war with Germany. Though we were ill prepared in 1939, the subsequent few years saw the military, and in particular the air force, grow in strength and equipment until final victory was achieved. The airfields of Nottinghamshire and Derbyshire were part of that process.

3

ASHBOURNE

National Grid Reference SK 198455, 9 miles NW of Derby

Doubtlessly, Derbyshire's claim to fame regarding the war was the Rolls-Royce establishment, for, unlike its neighbouring county of Nottinghamshire, it had very few wartime airfields of any significance; just two, in fact. One of them was Ashbourne, situated on the edge of the moors at one of the prettiest sites in the county. The area was inspected during 1941 as a possible bomber airfield. Whilst concerns were expressed then about its locality (close to a farm and a collection of cottages), in the end levelling of the ground went ahead. The main contractors, Lehane, McKenzie and Shand, moved in to construct the main runways and hard perimeter tracks. Once the ground work had been accomplished, the Unit Construction Company moved in to construct the buildings. One large problem was immediately overcome when the farm previously mentioned, seen to be a hazard for aircraft taking off and landing and called 'Roadmeadow Farm', was promptly demolished in the name of safety.

Consideration was also given to a satellite airfield at Darley Moor. This came under scrutiny as to its suitability but again, a contractor, William Monk of Warrington, arrived to begin levelling the ground and laying runways.

Like most of the airfields within the East Midlands, Ashbourne was built to bomber airfield standards with three runways. The longest was 1,700 yards long with the remaining two 1,540 yards and 1,340 yards respectively. Construction began in the spring of

1941 and the airfield opened during the summer of 1942. When finished, Ashbourne came under the wing of No 92 Group. Owing to a period of expansion and re-organisation within Bomber Command and a prolonged spell of bad weather conditions, neither Ashbourne nor its satellite, Darley Moor, ever became operational bomber stations. With a change to No 93 Group authorised, a headquarters was set up at Egginton Hall, a country mansion on the banks of the River Dove, with a signal being sent to Ashbourne to the effect that it was to become a training airfield and the home of No 81 OTU.

Advance parties were soon arriving at the newly established airfield, including the first CO, Sqn Ldr Boston. He was accompanied by Plt Offs Holt and Blundell, together with one Warrant Officer, three NCOs and thirty other ranks. Motor vehicles in abundance were arriving every day: re-fuelling bowsers, ambulances, tractors – all that was essential to get an airfield up and operational. However, even at this late stage, some of the accommodation and technical buildings were not finished and various dignitaries arrived to view the building progress. Neither had any of the essential items, the aircraft, yet arrived and it would be several more months before they would do so. Bomber Command was suffering from a lack of modern aircraft and the failure of the twin-engined Avro Manchester to

A T2 hangar and ablutions block near the East/West runway.
(M. L. Giddings)

41

realise its expectations had hindered progress in the bombing campaign. For Ashbourne, however, a complement of 29 Wellingtons were allocated to 81 OTU to be used for training crews for Bomber Command, with an additional satellite airfield to be established at Church Broughton, about 8 miles south.

All military decisions in wartime were prone to change and the orders received at Ashbourne with regard to the OTU were certainly no exception! It was decided that the unit would be better suited being stationed at Whitchurch Heath in Shropshire and to receive the ageing Whitley instead of the Wellington. Its replacement at Ashbourne would be an Army Co-Operation unit and the airfield would lose its second satellite airfield, at Church Broughton, to Lichfield. Yet again another change took place when it was decided that Whitchurch Heath should be renamed Tilstock.

Without really having got started, Ashbourne went into a period similar to Care and Maintenance. September saw a transfer from No 93 Group to No. 70 Group Army Co-Operation Command and the arrival of a new CO, Sqn Ldr Peers. It was now known that the new unit was to be No.42 OTU, who were to travel up from Andover in Hampshire to their new base during October 1942. With a favourable weather report, the first aircraft, a Westland Lysander, left the south of England for Ashbourne. Its arrival, and that of those that followed, attracted a great deal of local interest and villagers from the neighbouring hamlets lined the Derby road to see the aircraft arrive. Once the Lysander had landed, the rest of the unit arrived in the form of Blenheims, Whitleys, Ansons and Oxfords. The following few days saw even greater inquisitive crowds as further aircraft and personnel began to arrive, including a party of WAAFs. On 22nd October, temporary command of Ashbourne was given to Wg Cdr Skelton as over 700 personnel began to settle into their new base. Once this was accomplished, a full flying training programme was set up as Ashbourne was deemed operational – a training airfield within No. 38 Group with a mandate to prepare crews for glider towing duties. Command of the airfield now passed to Gp Cpt The Lord Hamilton.

In all of the OTUs and training establishments, the unsus-pected would always happen, sometimes resulting in death. The first bad incident occurred at Ashbourne on 7th November when a Blenheim flown by Fg Off Mummery with LAC Clarke as crew hit a tree in the overshoot area. Immediately upon hitting the ground, the Blenheim burst into flames killing the airman, whilst Fg Off Mummery received severe injuries.

With crews still required for twin-engined medium bombers, Ashbourne became a very busy airfield for the rest of the year. That it was busy can be judged by the fact that in November one course comprised thirteen pilots, fifteen navigators, seven wireless operators and thirteen gunners to be trained before moving on to conversion courses or operational squadrons. Whilst the twin-engined aircraft used for training were adequate, the fact that they had been in service with other units for some considerable time, and had therefore accumulated high flying hours, obviously contributed to the accidents and aircraft failures. Incidents like that which occurred in January 1943, when the crew of a Blenheim perished as it appeared just to fall out of the sky for no apparent reason, happened all too often. Several days later another Blenheim had to make a forced landing without its undercarriage when a hydraulic oil pipe chaffed through. Whilst no lives were lost on this occasion, it showed that component failure was one of the main causes of accidents. The same month saw an Oxford crash land at Darley Moor when mechanical failure once again put the crew in jeopardy.

Despite these occurrences, training proceeded at a brisk pace. The Blenheims and Whitleys were, in the main, used to train pilots and navigators whilst the Ansons and Oxfords were used for wireless and gunnery training. Although the OTU was working at full pace, the need for more aircrew demanded a further increase in output. With the usual output from Ashbourne being nine crews per month, it was suggested that the station could easily provide sixteen. After being given a lot of thought, the matter was put on hold when, on 1st June 1943, Army Co-Operation Command was disbanded and absorbed into Technical Training Command. No 42 OTU was now to come under the umbrella of Fighter Command.

An inventory of the aircraft at 42 OTU carried out during June 1943 stated that the unit had on charge one Magister, one Hurricane, four Martinets, sixteen Ansons, 24 Blenheims and 25 Whitleys. During the same month, Darley Moor opened, allowing 'A' Flight to make it their permanent home.

A major accident on 8th July heralded the end of the Blenheims for training when a crash killed three crew members. For some time it had been thought that the Blenheims were becoming unreliable due to age and flying hours. Three days later the CO suspended all training on the type. It was never used again by 42 OTU and the training task was taken over by the Whitley Flight.

A change of CO came in August when Gp Cpt Hammond succeeded Gp Cpt The Lord Hamilton. With his arrival, rumours were abounding regarding a new type of aircraft to replace many of the OTU's ageing Blenheims and Whitleys. In September the rumours became fact with the arrival of the Armstrong Whitworth Albemarle. (See Operations Record Book copy.) Designed by Bristol, production moved to Armstrong Whitworth when the latter had spare design and production capacity. Though still only twin-engined, the type was placed in 'D' Flight, who felt it was a great improvement on the slower Whitleys. Darley Moor now became used for glider towing exercises after a Whitley successfully towed a Horsa glider out of the airfield. Further glider training came when the airfield and Ashbourne were transferred from 70 Group to 38 Group of the Second Tactical Air Force. More Albemarles were now arriving daily as the build-up to D-Day continued. Sadly the accident rate diminished only slightly with the new aircraft. By May 1944, the

Copy of ORB for Ashbourne station. The arrival of the new Albemarle on 5th September 1943. (PRO Air 29/679)

*A 38 Group Albermarle, with crew pictured around the time of D-Day.
(M. L. Giddings)*

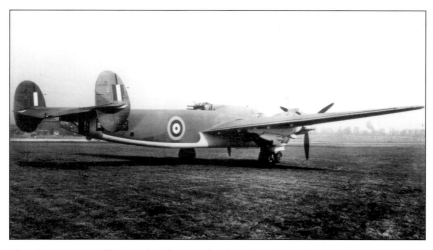

*The Armstrong Whitworth Albermarle showing the mid-upper turret.
(M. L. Giddings)*

situation had become so bad that engineers from the Bristol Aeroplane Company were called in to inspect the Hercules engines. They discovered that the porcelain base of the sparking plugs was breaking up under intense heat and had caused several of the engine failures.

Many of the crews that had trained at Ashbourne and Darley Moor took part in the invasion of Europe on the 6th June 1944. With a foothold on the Continent established, the AOC 38 Group sent a signal to Ashbourne stating that the 2,272 flying hours completed by 42 OTU from 6th June to September 1944 were exceptional. Crews trained at Ashbourne were again involved in the Arnhem operation but this was to be the last large-scale invasion they were to take part in. Yet again, tragedy reared its head just a few days before Christmas 1944 when an Albemarle crashed onto a house. Returning from a night exercise, it was on its final approach when it dropped suddenly and plunged earthwards. Immediately, local people rushed to the scene to help as the fire engines and ambulances from the station raced towards the ominous glow. Incredibly, the only death was that of the navigator, who had been thrown out of the aircraft as it crashed.

Christmas that year was celebrated in the usual style, but this time everyone knew that victory was close. Although flying

The one remaining flight hut pictured in 1975. (M. L. Giddings)

training began once again in the new year, it proved to be a very low key programme. On 20th January, a signal was received stating that 42 OTU were to be merged with 81 OTU, previous occupants of Ashbourne. The satellite airfield at Darley Moor would close, with the transfer of all personnel to an airfield in Lincolnshire. Yet again, the arrangement for 42 OTU to merge was rescinded and, instead, the OTU was disbanded on 20th March 1945 with Ashbourne closing down shortly after. No 28 MU moved in to store weapons on the site but when they moved in 1954 the curtain ran down on the station.

Around 1,400 aircrew were trained at Ashbourne and Darley Moor. It was stated in official circles that it could have been more but for the weather conditions at Ashbourne, standing as it did at 650 feet above sea level. Another factor was that with the continuing changes in aircraft, and the fact that most of the aircraft were nearly time expired, the expected flying hours could not be achieved. Both of these airfields did contribute greatly to the war effort but today there is very little left of either site to remind those of us interested in that period of their existence.

4

BALDERTON

National Grid Reference SK 816498, 3 miles SSE of Newark

It is well recorded that, sadly, Bomber Command losses during the Second World War were colossal. Though mainly caused by attacks from enemy fighters, enemy ground fire and flak damage, collision was another factor to be considered, given the very large numbers of bombers being sent on a single raid. In order to illustrate what could and did happen in many cases, let us look at just one such incident. The squadron was No.408 (Goose) of the Royal Canadian Air Force and the base was Balderton.

The night of 30th/31st May 1942 was to see the culmination of many months of planning at Bomber Command headquarters at High Wycombe, Buckinghamshire. A new C-in-C had arrived early in the year by the name of Air Marshal Arthur Harris. When presented with the figures relating to previous bombing raids over enemy territory he was appalled, for they showed that not one bomb in ten fell within five miles of its intended target. At this time the only targets were military installations or industrial areas but in February 1942, a new policy of bombing was instigated, in which aiming points were to be chosen in very large built-up areas, plus the introduction of saturation bombing. Air Marshal A T Harris had long advocated this method of bombing. In his mind he was already conceiving the destruction of a major German city by 1,000 bombers. Though several targets were considered worthy of attention, the final choice fell upon Cologne.

To raise 1,000 aircraft would entail all the commands with the

48

Air Marshal 'Bomber' Harris at his desk at Bomber Command in High Wycombe, with his Senior Air Staff Officer, Air Vice Marshal R. H. M. S. Saundby. (Crown)

exception of fighter, giving some squadrons over to Bomber Command for the raid. The task of assembling such a force would take about 48 hours and entail moving the aircraft to advance bases on the east coast. About 200 aircraft from Flying Training, Army Co-op, Coastal Command and the two Bomber Training Groups were involved including No 408 (Goose) Squadron, then equipped with the Handley Page Hampden medium bomber. Though originally based at Syerston, a detachment moved to Balderton on 9th December 1941 in preparation for the raid. From here they carried out training and awaited the details of the operation.

On the afternoon of 30th May, the groundcrews prepared the aircraft for the assault. Petrol tanks were filled up, bombs were loaded and ammunition for the guns was taken aboard. With the light fading, the crews arrived and boarded the Hampdens. As the flare path sprang into life, the aircraft taxied to the runway and one by one took off to join the main bomber force. Crossing the North Sea, the entire force approached Cologne. Flying one of the 408 Squadron aircraft was an Englishman, Flt Lt Brian Frow, who, unbeknown to him then, was to witness the sort of collision that most aircrew feared.

With a distance of 20 miles to run to the target, Flt Lt Frow and his crew were alert and watching for enemy aircraft as well as striving to maintain their position among so many other bombers. Flying a straight and level course, despite the flak that was coming up, the pilot suddenly saw a flash of tracer in front of him, followed by a loud explosion and intense light as one of the bombers some way ahead blew up. Despite being told that weaving was the best way to avoid being hit by either tracer or flak, Flt Lt Frow continued to hold his straight and level course. Not so for many others, who had also witnessed the explosion. They began to weave and dodge around the sky, attempting to dodge the shells that were now coming up. This was fatal as the crew of the Hampden saw a Stirling and a Wellington getting into a position that would endanger both aircraft. What happened next did so quickly as the Wellington came up underneath the Stirling and touched its tailplane, cutting it straight off. Both aircraft then seemed to rise together before, to the shock of the Hampden crew, the Wellington blew up. The Stirling lurched and dived to earth, its descent finishing in a ball of flame which was clearly seen by the Hampden crew. Stunned by what had

The crew of a Hampden from No 408 (Goose) Sqdn RCAF in September 1941. (408 Sqdn via V. Baker)

happened, the crew could only carry on and pray that the same did not happen to them. This incident was not the only one throughout a night that was to see the destruction of a German city.

Situated two miles south of Newark, Balderton began life as a satellite for No 25 OTU based at Finningley. Part of No 7 Group, the unit flew the Handley Page Hampden. Known to all airmen as 'the flying panhandle' due to its long slender fuselage and thin tail boom, it was the last of the twin-engined bombers to enter RAF service during the 1930s Expansion Period. Designed to Air Ministry Specification B.9/32 issued in September 1932, it seemed to hold out great promise for Bomber Command, being faster than the Whitley or Wellington as well as carrying a larger bomb load a greater distance. By 1941, however, it had been relegated to minor roles, including the training of pilots at OTUs.

Balderton transferred to No 5 Group in July and became a satellite to Syerston. On 9th December No 408 (Goose) Squadron of the Royal Canadian Air Force moved their Hampdens over from the parent station, sending a detachment to North

Pilot and co-pilot of a Hampden bomber, both grim-faced and determined.
(Crown)

Luffenham shortly afterwards. Settled in by Christmas, the squadron began bombing operations over Germany as the new year arrived, heralding a new sense of urgency for Bomber Command.

It was Arthur Harris, the tough Commander-in-Chief of the command, who stated that one 'could not win wars by defending oneself'. Since the Battle of Britain had been fought and won, Bomber Command had carried the war forward by relentlessly attacking Germany, much of it without any success in hitting a specific target despite the propaganda machine working full-time to convince us that this was not so. All of this changed on 22nd February 1942 when Harris took control.

As we have read in the opening paragraphs, he brought with him the idea that selective target bombing did not appear to be working but area bombing with vast formations would work. It came as a shock to him upon taking command to be told that only about 375 bombers were available at any one time. Two and a half years into the war and the strength of the command had hardly changed since 1939! There was one aspect of hope on the horizon, which came in the form of a radio aid to navigation and blind bombing known as Gee. This was a medium range radio aid in which ground transmitters in the UK sent a signal that was received by the aircraft, enabling it to plot its course more accurately. By 1942 the gradual re-equipment of four-engined bombers with the device was gathering apace. The first attack using Gee took place on 8th March 1942 with an attack on Essen. Whilst it did improve the navigation for the crew, it fell a long way short of the answer to the problem. All of this further helped to convince Arthur Harris that his method was the ultimate answer to bringing Germany to its knees. At the earliest opportunity he put forward his thoughts to Air Vice Marshal Robert Saundby, his deputy commander. 'How long will it be before we can muster a really crushing force, something like a thousand?'

'We could do it now' was his answer.

'Rubbish' retorted Harris.

'But we could' answered Saundby, 'if we make use of the conversion and training planes. Then there are the bombers we transferred to Coastal Command. That would push us within reach of a thousand.'

Harris pondered, grinned and said, 'We'll try it. We've got to try it. We'll start working it out tomorrow.'

With the 1,000 bomber raids, the risk of collision was always there. This photo shows a Halifax III with its front end taken away. In a collision with another Halifax, the navigator and bomb aimer, not wearing clip-on parachutes, sadly fell to their deaths. (PRO Air 14/1443)

So it was that with all the aircraft put together, all the instructor pilots from the OTUs and conversion units and the regular bomber squadrons, the 1,000 bomber plan was conceived. No 408 Squadron were part of that first raid on Cologne and, as the opening paragraphs of the chapter suggest, the risk of collision with so many aircraft in a particular area of airspace was very real. Fortunately a system of staggering the aircraft was later implemented to minimise this risk.

With a resident bomber squadron, it soon became apparent that Balderton needed hard runways. In September 1942 work began on their construction but such was the upheaval that No 408 Squadron moved to Leeming in Yorkshire. The work at the base took until August 1943 but when completed it enabled Balderton to accommodate almost any type of aircraft of the period. Constructed to a typical Bomber Command configuration, it had three runways, one of which was 6,000 feet long, a second was 4,620 feet long and a third 4,390 feet long. An asphalt perimeter track around the airfield gave way to many dispersal

A Hampden bomber and crews return from a raid. (Crown)

areas. Immediately prior to the completion of the runway work, the base had been used to store Airspeed Horsa gliders in preparation for the airborne landings in occupied Europe.

Balderton did not re-open fully until well into 1943, but in March of that year a different sound of aero engine was to be heard. This was the Gloster Meteor, which was powered by a Rolls-Royce built W2B/23 turbo-jet designed by Sir Frank Whittle. (See the chapter on Rolls-Royce.) The aircraft was the fifth prototype to be built and used Balderton for two or three weeks for taxiing and flight trials.

With the hard runways it became possible for a permanent unit to move in and on 15th August 1943 No 1668 Heavy Conversion Unit formed, equipped with sixteen Lancasters and sixteen Halifaxes. The second of the large four-engined bombers, the Halifax had the dubious honour of being the first of its sort to drop bombs on Germany. However, due to rising losses on Bomber Command operations, and the increased flow of Lancasters to the squadron, from September 1943 some of them found their way to the OTUs and HCUs. Their time at Balderton was limited and by November they had left and the sound of heavy bombers was replaced by the Bristol Blenheims of No 12 (P)AFU. Every day during December would find them practising circuits and bumps. For this month alone, the locals would have grounds to grumble about the noise when flying was from dawn to dusk. This usage did, however, prove only temporary for Balderton had been earmarked to become a major base for the United States Army Air Force.

In December 1941, the US Army Air Forces had 71 operational groups consisting of 27 bombardment, 24 pursuit 11 observation, six transport, two composite and one photographic. One day later, three weeks after the United States had been forced into the war by the Japanese, the Prime Minister, Winston Churchill, arrived in Washington DC aboard HMS Duke of York. Pre-arranged meetings with President Roosevelt had brought him to the capital for an agenda which included a brief stating that the war effort against Germany was to take priority over the fight against Japan. During the meetings it was agreed that the United States was to establish an army air force in Britain to mount raids against industrial targets in Germany and occupied Europe. It was formally agreed that the units conceived would become known as the 9th Air Force and would primarily include bombardment (heavy) and fighter groups as well as some bombardment (medium), reconnaissance and troop carrier groups plus support units. One of the troop carrier groups was the 437th, which arrived in Britain in January 1944 and was re-formed at Army Air Force Station 482 – Balderton.

Although constituted on 15th April 1943, the group was not activated until 1st May of the same year. The next eight months were spent in the USA training with C-46 and C-47 aircraft in preparation for duty overseas and becoming an integral part of the 9th Air Force. Meanwhile the configuration of Balderton had been brought up to a Class A airfield. Although the RAF had increased the size and capacity of the airfield, it was still not large enough to accommodate an entire carrier group. Further and larger hangars were built to provide cover for major aircraft overhauls, together with more technical blocks and workshops. Large underground fuel dumps were dug out and extra administration offices and accommodation blocks were built comprising both hutted and brick built units. The Horsa gliders that had been stored at Balderton were now put to use in the training role as the C-46s and C-47s (Dakotas) arrived from America. Despite all this work, however, it was never intended that the 436th TCG would remain at Balderton and on 5th February 1944 they moved to their permanent wartime base at Ramsbury, to be replaced by the 439th TCG on 21st February.

During this early part of 1944, the plans for an allied invasion of the French channel coast were at an advanced stage. On 2nd January, General Sir Bernard Montgomery had arrived back in Britain to take command of the Allied Land Forces under the overall command of General Dwight D Eisenhower, the Supreme Commander. This invasion of NW Europe was to be the most ambitious enterprise of the war so far. In order to keep the troops detailed for the operation informed of every move, General Montgomery visited every troop stronghold and every airfield connected with the invasion. All were impressed by his confidence and style and the manner in which he explained to them the way the operation was intended to go. However, despite his confidence, Winston Churchill asked, 'Why are we doing this?', believing inwardly that the operation could easily misfire. Not so the Americans, who were anxious to hit at the enemy on the Continent as soon as possible. This difference in feeling, even up to the eve of D-Day, caused friction between the military commands of both countries.

No such feeling was apparent, however, at Balderton as the air echelon of the 439th TCG arrived on 21st February 1944 with four squadrons of C-47s followed by the ground echelon on 11th March. They had been preceeded by several other US units, including the 1070th Signal Company Service Group, which had moved to Balderton from Coggeshall in Essex on 21st February 1944.

There now began a period of extensive training in the towing of gliders, yet, for some reason, the 439th were ordered to leave Balderton and move south to Upottery. By 24th April the move had been accomplished, but the unit was destined to return to the airfield and take part in Operation 'Market', the airborne operation of 'Market Garden'.

Balderton now entered a period of relative calm disturbed only by the Lancasters of No 5 Lancaster Finishing School, who used it for circuits and bumps. The airfield was to play no part in Operation 'Overlord', which began on the 6th June 1944. For that month and the following, whilst history was being made, very little use was made of the up-graded facilities at the airfield. All of this changed, however, during the first weeks of September, when the ground echelon of the 439th TCG arrived back. They were followed by the air echelon, now under the command of Colonel Charles H Young. Once again the sound of Pratt and Whitney engines carried throughout the entire area as plans were formulated for the 439th to take part in Operation 'Market'. Balderton suddenly had become a front line station in carrying the war back to the enemy as the push to Berlin began.

Despite General Eisenhower's own plans not agreeing with that of Montgomery, the latter was not to give his ideas up easily. Montgomery had conceived a plan to advance to the Ruhr and the heart of German industry by either of two routes. One ran due east, which would incur a battle to breach the Siegfried Line. The other ran NNE towards Arnhem. At a point near Cleve the Siegfried Line ended, and if Arnhem could be secured, the line could be outflanked. This north route crossed Holland and was a far more difficult option. To reach Arnhem by this route it would be necessary to cross three wide canals and the Maas and Waal rivers. Once across the Lower Rhine at Arnhem, Montgomery intended to advance east towards Osnabruck, Munster and Hamm and on into the Ruhr. This would have been the second part of the operation code-named 'Garden'. Exactly what happened is told simply yet accurately by a journalist of the time and is recorded here verbatim with his permission.

'The British were advancing into Holland from the south, entering a country bad in autumn for tank warfare due to the muddy conditions. A crossing of the River Maas had been forced, but beyond the river the enemy held the town of Eindhoven in the open plain; beyond Eindhoven were the two main branches of the Rhine, the Waal and the Lek, both great rivers spanned by steel bridges. On the near side of the Waal lay Nijmegen; five miles to the north was the little town of Elst; five miles beyond that flows the Lek, on the farther bank of which stood Arnhem. It was decided to drop thousands of paratroops to seize Nijmegen, Eindhoven and Arnhem. With these crossings secure, British armour would then rush across the bridges, fan out into Westphalia and thus with one stroke turn the defence system that protected western Germany. On September 17th 1944, this plan was attempted.

'That September day saw more paratroops than had ever been seen before in one air-borne operation. Eindhoven fell fairly easily but Nijmegen yielded only after a sharp struggle. Simultaneously, spearheads of the British army moved forward across the Dutch frontier; the whole point of the scheme was that the link-up between the main army and the air-borne men should be effected without delay. By 10 am on September 18th, troops of the British Second Army had made contact with the air-borne troops at Eindhoven and on the 20th they were smashing through to the River Waal, north-east of Nijmegen as the city itself was the scene of a furious battle. A vast armada of gliders, filling the sky for 285 miles, swept out of Britain with reinforcements, with the Halifaxes and Stirlings acting as tug planes. Meanwhile, the Germans were reacting with furious determination. At Arnhem, about 6,500 men had floated down by parachute and succeeded in gaining control of the bridge, together with an area about two miles square. By day and night they experienced frantic enemy counter attacks. The time factor began to turn against them, for the main British forces, advancing from Nijmegen, encountered stiff enemy resistance at Elst. On September 23rd, thousands of British and American glider-borne troops were dropped in support of the British Second Army's efforts to relieve the Arnhem men. At the same time the Germans

59

made repeated efforts to cut the Allied corridor to Nijmegen. Sadly, no reinforcements reached the paratroops; the RAF in bad weather, continued to take frightful risks to drop supplies but steadily the tiny garrison were being decimated as the Germans, recovered from their first shock, rushed up tanks, mortars and self-propelled guns. Eventually the airborne men were split up into small bodies and though still fighting, the enemy ring around them slowly contracted. By September 25th it was apparent that the bid had failed and that there could be no link-up between the main army and the vanguard at Arnhem. During the nights of the 25th and 26th, the survivors slipped back through enemy lines and were taken back in boats. 2,800 were evacuated, and 1,200 wounded had to be left behind. Such was the tragedy of Arnhem.'

As the first part of the operation swung into action, a security cordon was thrown around Balderton. All leave was cancelled as aircraft and gliders were respectively fuelled and checked. As Sunday 17th September 1944 dawned, first light saw the C-47s lining the runway with the Waco CG-4A gliders strategically placed to be hooked up to the tug aircraft. Fifty aircraft with gliders were eventually to leave Balderton carrying men and artillery to Nijmegen. In addition the gliders carried para-troopers for the initial assault. Struggling to gain height, the armada crossed the English coastline and headed for Holland. With very little opposition, the drop and glider landings went ahead as planned and all aircraft returned safely to Balderton. The next day the 439th were airborne again, this time to drop supplies to the troops fighting below. As they flew over the drop zones the signs of a desperate struggle below were becoming obvious. The main land advance had stalled as the enemy ground fire became intense. History records that although the British division held the Arnhem bridge for four days, the entire operation was doomed to failure due to bad planning. The 1st Airborne lost 6,400 men, 1,200 being killed and the rest taken prisoner. Five VCs were awarded, four of them posthumously. When the outcome of the operation became known at Balderton it was an air of despondency that settled throughout the group.

Following the failure of 'Market Garden', orders were received at Balderton that the 439th were to move onto the Continent in preparation for assisting in Operation 'Varsity', the crossing of the Rhine. Amidst a great deal of confusion, the 439th ground and air echelons had left Balderton by 23rd September. Almost immediately after their departure, the airfield reverted back to Bomber Command and No.5 Group. Wasting no time at all, No.227 Squadron flew in from Bardney equipped with Lancasters Mks I and III. The squadron had been formed from a nucleus of 'A' flight of No.9 Squadron and 'B' flight of No.619 Squadron. After reforming at Bardney on 7th October 1944, they moved to Balderton on the 12th. Immediately the ground and aircrews had settled in the buildings recently vacated by the Americans operations began with bombing sorties to many of the German cities, among them Munich and Gravenhorst.

For the local villagers, the night was always disturbed as the Lancasters, heavy with bombs and fuel, roared at rooftop height above their houses. Then there was silence until they began to return in the early hours of the next morning. As time went on, many local people would count the aircraft out and count them back in again. Many did not return and the sadness of such instances was felt as much by the local populace as on the station itself.

The squadron remained until 5th April 1945, when it moved to Strubby in Lincolnshire. Silence reigned and two weeks later Balderton was placed under Care and Maintenance. By 1st June it had been transferred to No.40 Group Maintenance Command (55 Wing) with No.1 Equipment Disposal Depot forming the same day. Re-designated No.254 Maintenance Unit on 14th June 1945, it disbanded on 8th July 1946 and became a sub-site of No.255 MU at Fulbeck until 30th November 1948, when that unit disbanded into No.98 MU at Wickenby, now storing ammunition. In 1951 Newton became the parent unit and Balderton continued as a storage depot until 30 August 1955, when it once again returned to Care and Maintenance. With signs of what was to become known as 'the Cold War' apparent, the runways of Balderton were used to store 4,000lb bombs. When they were removed so ended the final use of the airfield, and with the construction of the Newark A1 bypass its destruction began. From the ground it is still possible to find small sections of the airfield, but it is from the air that the outline of Balderton is apparent.

5

BIRCOTES

National Grid Reference SK642940, 1 mile W of Bawtry on the A631

Whilst only a grass airfield, this airfield had a short but very intensive and mixed life. Located immediately west of the town of Bawtry (after which it was sometimes called) it was never an operational airfield but fulfilled a support role. Opened in November 1941, well after the Battle of Britain and at a time when the UK was opening a new airfield every three days, Bircotes was utility to say the least. The three grass runways were symmetrical, with one running N/S 18/36 1,540 yards long, another E/W 09/27 ten yards shorter and another SE/NW at 1,350 yards long. Additionally there were 30 circular hard-standings for dispersing the aircraft. Hangarage, the larger two of which still stand in 2003, comprised one T2 type, one B1 type and one blister; accommodation was available for 764 RAF and 80 WAAF.

The first aircraft to use Bircotes were from No 25 OTU, based up the road at Finningley, which used this airfield and Balderton as satellites. The unit flew a variety of Wellingtons, Manchesters and Ansons for multi-engine training and crew training for entire bomber crews. As was common to many airfields in this area Bircotes and Balderton were training bases; the parent unit was always over-committed, requiring satellite bases for circuit training and often night flying training where all three bases could be used simultaneously thereby giving more crews training in safer, and quieter conditions. Ground training was also undertaken here with ground instruction buildings, link trainers, machine gun ranges and a crew procedure trainer.

Bircotes remained in this role until January 1943, when 25 OTU disbanded. However, the utilisation increased for two months from August 1943 when No 82 OTU also used it as a satellite for its Wellington, three Martinets and two Tomahawks, the latter being for fighter affiliation exercises. Again, 82 OTU was a bomber conversion unit so the local residents would not have noticed the additional aircraft as they were all the same type. The 82 OTU aircraft returned to Ossington in October but were immediately replaced with even more Wellingtons from 18 OTU, which had its HQ at Bramcote and used several satellites, including Bircotes, from March 1943 to November 1944. Another Wellington unit, 18 OTU kept the circuit and ground building busy with one or two flights operating almost independently.

Bombers were not the only types seen as No 16 FTS at Newton shared Bircotes from February 1942 to August 1943 for pilot training with Master IIIs, Oxfords and a sprinkling of Ansons. Bircotes was used for day flying practice.

The town of Bawtry was the home of HQ No 1 Group, Bomber Command and being only 1 mile away Bircotes naturally became the home of No 1 Group Communications Flight, which formed here on 20 July 1941 for transporting high ranking officers around their Group stations. Thus, the types based here were varied, including Avro Tutor, Proctor, Leopard Moth, Lysander, Anson and Tiger Moth. The Flight migrated to Finningley for three months from January 1943 but then settled back at Bircotes until November 1945, when the airfield closed for flying.

Flying was not the only RAF activity at Bircotes as three Maintenance Units used it at various times: No 35 MU at Heywood, Lancashire used it from November 1944 until well into 1945 for the storage of aircraft equipment; No 61 MU from Handforth, Cheshire used it from November 1944 until July 1948, also for aircraft equipment, and No 250 MU actually formed here on 12 June 1945 as an MT storage unit, remaining until it disbanded on 31st December 1946 with its role being absorbed into No 61 MU, with which it shared the facilities.

With the shrinkage of the post-war RAF and the storage of material being reduced, Bircotes was vacated in July 1948 and soon de-requisitioned by the RAF and returned to agriculture. The two large hangars are still used for storage but there is no trace of the airfield except for the treeless area it originally covered giving a clue as to its former role.

6

BURNASTON

National Grid Reference SK290303, 5 miles SW of Derby

During the expansion period of the mid-1930s, it became apparent to the Air Ministry that if war did eventually come, the country would be woefully short of pilots and aircrew. A vast training scheme swung into action aided by countries of the Commonwealth. Among these was Australia, who, during the early part of the war, offered help to Great Britain with the Empire Air Training Scheme. Overall this scheme provided 50,000 trained aircrew each year. The Royal Australian Air Force formed 17 squadrons in the UK and the Middle East. New Zealand and Canada also contributed substantially to the scheme, many individual aircrew flying with RAF squadrons but with a shoulder flash on their uniform denoting their country of origin. The Empire Air Training Scheme ran parallel to that of the RAF, which utilised the civilian operated Elementary and Reserve Training Schools, with many airfields accommodating such units. One of them was Burnaston in Derbyshire, now more commonly known as Derby Airport. The latter name had actually been mooted before the Second World War began, when, on Saturday 13th June 1939, the airfield had been opened as Derby's Municipal Airport. At the opening ceremony by the Secretary of State for Air, Sir Kingsley Wood, hundreds of people arrived to watch a flying display at the little airfield which had been established several years previously and was already the home of the RAF Volunteer Reserve Training Centre.

A product of the University Air Squadrons, whose concept dated back to 1925, it was not until May 1939 that the original University Air Squadrons were absorbed into the RAFVR. Conceived in January 1937, the RAFVR existed to provide continuous flying training for pilots who had completed their full time service but who had been placed on the reserve list. By early 1939, with the obvious signs of a world war developing, it was expanded to accommodate the training of civilians. The aim was to provide a reserve of 2,400 pilots capable of supporting the regular air force. Using many airfields, including Burnaston, and the local flying clubs that were *in situ*, it set about training pilots who were mainly available only at weekends. With their training taking twice as long as a regular RAF unit's, it soon became apparent that the target number of reserve pilots was not going to be reached in the time required. The government of the day therefore proposed the expansion of reserve training units, which resulted in the formation of the civilian run Elementary and Reserve Flying Training Schools and the Civil Air Guard.

It was No 30 E&RFTS that formed at Burnaston on 29th

The first step for any would-be pilot – the Link Trainer at Burnaston – No 30 E&RFTS gave many pilots initial training. (Derby Library)

September 1938. Flying training was open to medically fit young men between the ages of 18 and 25 who were educated to School Certificate standard. Upon joining they were given the rank of Sergeant and, of course, were taught to fly at no cost. When this free training became generally known, the would-be pilots left the flying clubs, where they had to pay for flying tuition, to join the E&RFTS. So many did leave that the government allowed the flying clubs to become part of a new organisation called the Civil Air Guard. With this method they subsidised very heavily the cost that a student would be expected to pay at a flying club. However, there was one stipulation – that if required, the trainees would give their services to *any* branch of the armed services when asked to do so.

On the outbreak of war, No 30 E&RFTS, which had been running very successfully at Burnaston under the civilian organisation Air Schools Ltd, came under military control. The director of Air Schools, Captain N Roy Harben DFC, assisted by an ex-RAF officer, E W Phillips, had also formed the Derby Aero Club at Burnaston. They were sad to see the training school go from their control, but

'Now, you start the engine by swinging the prop.' Students at No 30 E&RFTS at Burnaston, 1939. (Derby Library)

with the threat of war coming ever closer it had become necessary to bring the club under Air Ministry regulations.

No 30 E&RFTS was equipped with the usual selection of training aircraft available over this period. Tiger Moths, Miles Magisters and Hawker Harts were now to be seen for long periods over the local area. The pupils were signed on initially for a period of five years and all were then given the rank of Sergeant pilots. They were obliged to report for regular service as soon as war became imminent and were paid the sum of 10 shillings per day (50p) during their training, this increasing to 12 shillings and sixpence (62½p) when trained and given their wings. In the case of the Civil Air Guard, the pupils were also given a one-piece flying suit.

Burnaston and No 30 E&RFTS soon settled into a training routine. As the threat of war edged even closer, the training became more intense and the Air Ministry announced amongst other changes that all the E&RFTSs would drop the term 'reserve' and become just EFTS.

And so Burnaston went to war. On the eve, it was a hushed

Three student pilots of No 30 E&RFTS, Burnaston. Note the 'Sidcot Type' flying suits. (Derby Library)

scene as all personnel listened to Chamberlain's broadcast. Each had their own thoughts. Was an invasion imminent, as had happened to most of the European mainland? As if proof were needed that this thought was certainly in the minds of the Air Ministry, orders were received to fit bomb racks under the wings of all training aircraft. Such was the desperation at the time.

As the country entered the period of the Phoney War, life at Burnaston appeared to carry on as normal. Due to a move from No 26 Group to No 50 Group, No 30 EFTS was re-numbered No 16 EFTS on 10th April 1940 and was allocated a Relief Landing Ground at Battlestead Hill with another at Abbots Bromley in Staffordshire. Later an Emergency Landing Ground was established at Birchwood Park near Ashbourne. Still a grass airfield, Burnaston was expanded to a four runway pattern with the maximum length of the main one being 1,000 yards.

As the Battle of Britain was being fought over Kent and Sussex, the training of pilots continued. The battle was beginning to enter its second phase as the end of July approached and the attacks on military airfields increased. Sunday 28th July dawned fine and remained fair until early evening, when the cloud increased. Using this cloud cover, a lone raider dropped a stick of bombs on the airfield, resulting in some damage but no loss of life or aircraft. The first of several minor attacks on the airfield, it brought the reality of war closer to the trainees and their instructors.

With the Battle of Britain fought and won, thoughts were very slowly turning to taking the war across the Channel in order to defeat the enemy. Any invasion of the Continent would demand massed forces and the means of their transportation would have to be various. Thus it was that the formation of the Glider Pilot Regiment became one of the factors of this undertaking. It performed a duty that was a major part of the wartime airborne operations and Burnaston was destined to become part of the organisation.

The regiment owed its formation to Winston Churchill, who, on 26th April 1941, visited the Central Landing Establishment at Ringway, near Manchester, which had been set up to train paratroops and glider pilots for combat. Churchill was shocked by the lack of men under training and immediately resolved to increase Britain's airborne forces.

In 1942, the regiment comprised two battalions, one

commanded by Lieutenent Colonel Iain Murray DSO and the other by Lieutenant Colonel John Place. Two wings were established, each having six squadrons comprising four flights. Glider pilots were drawn from all units of the army to undergo an aircrew selection board. When passed they progressed to an RAF EFTS such as Burnaston to undergo Link Trainer experience before receiving flying training on the Tiger Moth. From here they proceeded to a glider training school for flying training on the Hotspur glider. They would then move to a Glider Conversion Unit for similar on the Airspeed Horsa, the main combatant glider. Although trained by the RAF to be pilots, the men selected for the regiment were also trained combat soldiers able to play their part in the land attack once they had landed the glider safely. Burnaston now became one of the foremost stations in teaching army personnel to fly. As the RAF blue mixed with the army khaki, it became apparent to all personnel that, although Britain was then maintaining a defensive stance, plans were being formulated for an ultimate invasion of Europe.

The army pupils arrived at Burnaston with their regimental shoulder flash with the winged horse Pegasus on the upper arm. They launched into a period of intensive basic pilot training, usually consisting of a 10-hour flying course. As we have already read, once they had completed several solo flights with No.16 EFTS, they then moved on to a glider training school before going to a HGCU for conversion to the heavy gliders.

No 16 EFTS continued with its training duties alongside the glider pilots. Due to the increase in pilot training, the new RLG at Battlestead Hill was brought into further use on 15th May 1942. Each day would see the yellow Tiger Moths or Magisters flying from Burnaston to either of the RLGs, where they would practise circuits and bumps. This continued to be the main role of Burnaston until the end of the war.

Suddenly the need for pilots diminished and flying activity at the airfield declined rapidly. In 1947, No 16 EFTS was stood down, only to take on a new role as No 16 Reserve Flying School. The unit was formed to train RAFVR pilots of No.65 Reserve Centre with much of the flying still being done on the Tiger Moth, although two Avro Ansons were recorded as being on strength. The name 'Derby Aero Club' was revived together with 'Air Schools Ltd', who formed Derby Aviation, which became involved in buying, selling and maintaining aeroplanes. By 1951 the venerable Tiger Moth had been replaced by the Percival Prentice whilst a new unit, No 3 Basic Flying Training School, was formed with the DeHavilland Chipmunk. By 1953, both the flying schools had closed down but a scheduled civilian service between Burnaston and Jersey ensured that the airfield remained flying. The aircraft used was a Dragon Rapide twin-engined biplane and with Ostend then included in the schedules, more and larger aircraft were required. They came in the form of the Dakota and, in 1955, the Miles Marathon. Conversion work was also carried out on several Mosquito B.35s, the first such aircraft to fly into Burnaston.

The next four years saw the airfield flourish and become very busy, but as Burnaston was a grass airfield, this use was bound to take its toll on its surface; so much so that it was decided to close Burnaston and concentrate instead on the old wartime airfield at Castle Donington (now East Midlands Airport.) In a final flourish, a Canadair Argonaut landed to demonstrate to Derby Airways that four-engined aircraft were the future, but, sadly, this was not the case for Burnaston. Before leaving, Derby

A rare photo of a Magister I (L5959/A) of No 16 EFTS at Burnaston. (Andy Thomas)

Airways changed its name to British Midland, a name that survives today. Gradually the airfield fell into decay and, although the CAA issued a new licence for flying to be resumed, the Conservative Government of the time felt that the land would be better used by industry. Accordingly, they sold the airfield to the Toyota car company of Japan, who built the largest car factory in the UK on the site.

It is not recorded how many students obtained their wings whilst flying from Burnaston. What is known is that many went on to become pilots in all the RAF commands and, in that respect, the airfield played its part admirably.

7

CHURCH BROUGHTON

National Grid Reference SK215320, approximately 2 miles SE of Sudbury, adjacent to the A50

Started in 1942 this satellite airfield in No 93 Group (Operational training) in Bomber Command (with its HQ at Eggington Hall, Derby) was first used in August 1942 when No 27 OTU at Lichfield utilised it as a satellite instead of Tatenhill. Tatenhill was not suitable for Wellington aircraft.

Built on the usual three runway layout with runways 1,900, 1,400 and 1,350 yards in length, the station had one T2 hangar, one B1 hangar and 27 heavy bomber hardstandings and accommodation for 1,274 RAF and 156 WAAF personnel. As soon as the B1 type hangar was constructed, 'B' Flight arrived with Wellington Ic aircraft to operate exclusively from here, keeping the HQ and other flights at Lichfield. 'B' Flight was subsequently joined by 'D' Flight as the size and strength of the station developed.

No 27 OTU had formed at Lichfield on 23rd April 1941 with Wellingtons to train night bomber crews. The usual intensive flying in both day and night time was carried out with new personnel training as a crew before moving to an operational squadron or to a conversion unit for another type of bomber. Many Australians were trained here and at Lichfield. Church Broughton was commanded by a Squadron Leader until Sqn Ldr Warren was promoted to Wing Commander as CO of Church Broughton on 29 March 1943. The airfield had good night flying lighting and it is recorded that when an American aircraft landed at night with the aid of roof sodium lights the pilot stated that it was doubtful whether he would have been able to land without their assistance.

Aircraft from 27 OTU took part in raids on Düsseldorf on 10th September 1942, Bremen on 13th and on Essen three nights later with ten, fourteen and twelve Wellingtons respectively. It is not recorded which flew from Church Broughton. There were no casualties on the first raid, but on the second, one plane crashed on take off, another shortly after take off, another went missing over enemy territory and one crashed on landing back at base. On the third night one failed to return and on another occasion the crew bailed out but none were hurt.

Tatenhill was given up totally by Lichfield on 7th November 1942 and the accidents continued, as at all training stations. Wellington N2511 had a fire when starting up on 27th October; Mk III Z1744 crashed two miles from the airfield on 20th November, killing the crew; BJ834 had a port engine fire on 23rd December but safely landed. Accidents continued into 1943 with

An all too familiar sight around Nottinghamshire and Derbyshire – an OTU's Wellington that came down on a private residence. (SE Newspapers)

73

BK241x crashing four miles NE of the airfield, killing Sgt Bell and his crew; Mk III BJ989 had its port wheel catch a hole left by the contractors, causing considerable damage on 16th April; Mk III X3998 suffered a port engine failure whilst on a bombing trip from here and the undercarriage collapsed on landing back at base; Mk III BK199 crash landed on 17th June; BK453 undershot and landed short of the runway on 27th June; BJ784 made a heavy landing on 4th July; BJ713 had its starboard engine cut on take off and in the resulting crash two of the crew were killed; X3727 crash landed on 3rd September with no injuries and BK195 swung off the runway on landing on 22nd September, again with no injuries.

For senior students, nickelling and bombing raids continued, including Nantes on 11th June 1943, Paris on 13th June, Rouen and Rheims on 20th June, Paris on 22nd, Tours on 26th, Le Mans on 1st July, Orleans on 5th, Laval on 12th; and these continued almost every other night for many months with virtually no losses. Bigger raids followed when on 2nd September eight Wellingtons bombed Foret Mormal, France and nine bombed Bolougne on the 8th. Usual bomb loads were seven 500lb bombs carried by the Mk III aircraft and eight 500lb bombs by the Mk Xs.

Two USAAF aircraft landed at this airfield on 30th April 1944 to bring wounded US soldiers to the 108th General Hospital, which must have been close by. General Lee, Deputy to General Eisenhower, visited here by air on 22 May and later proceeded to the US Army camp at Sudbury. Wing Commander K D Baird DFC arrived as Satellite CO at Church Broughton on 3rd June and a cricket match between Lichfield and Church Broughton ended in disaster with Lichfield being 160 for 4 after Church Broughton were 36 all out! By October 1944 the ammunition held in the bomb store was reduced to practice bombs, flame floats and similar for training purposes and small arms ammunition with bombs no longer held.

Unfortunately, fatal accidents continued with HZ533 crashing at the end of the runway on 18 December 1944 killing the crew. In 22nd January 1945 HQ No 91 group took over the airfield from No 93 Group and it ceased to be an exclusive RAAF OTU. With Bomber Command losses dropping, the task of the OTUs was very slowly quietening down. Minor accidents continued but there were no fatalities at Church Broughton during 1945.

The staff were still predominantly Australian, with the station Admin Officer, Sqn Ldr J E Pyke, RAAF being posted out in March. He was subsequently replaced by another RAAF Sqn Ldr and the Australian Flight Commander of 'D' Flight was replaced by an RAF officer, Sqn Ldr B R Wilson, on 23rd March. The very last detail of the OTU was flown one week behind schedule on 22nd June 1945 and by 30th June the rear party had closed their operations at Church Broughton and No 27 OTU ceased to exist from 8th July 1945.

The airfield's use diminished but it did not close. 27 OTU had been joined by No 1429 (Czech) Operational Training Flight from Woolfox Lodge on 26th August 1942 in No 93 Group, also flying Wellington bombers training Czech crews. This unit moved to Thornaby on 8th November 1942. A third unit formed here in May 1943 as No 93 Group Screened Instructors' Pool, also flying Wellingtons under the command of Sqn Ldr K S Stammers DFM. The unit formed to reduce the fatal accident rate in bomber OTUs. . . Screened instructors were those who had completed one or more operational tours and were therefore 'screened' or protected from further operations. The six instructors in this unit had trained 550 students by the time it disbanded at Leicester East in October 1944, having moved there from Church Broughton in April 1944.

Church Broughton was also used by Rolls-Royce, who had an experimental flight called Flight Trials Unit here for testing their jet engines, which were being developed under very secret conditions. This unit took over the MAP hangar on 10th April and moved in from Balderton on 28th April 1944, ultimately returning to Hucknall in 1946 when this airfield closed for flying. Some engines were test flown under Wellingtons, hence merging in well with the large number of those resident. This lends credibility to the story about an American B-17 crew's astonishment when flying alongside a Wellington: when the B-17 pilot opened up the throttles to leave the Wellington behind, the latter stopped one engine, feathered the propeller and stayed with the B-17; the B-17 went flat out, the Wellington stopped the other engine and then proceeded to accelerate away from the amazed Americans as if on no engines, as they could not see the jet engine slung under the bomb bay!

The early Meteor jet fighter was developed here with Rolls-Royce from April 1944 until they closed in 1946. The first flight of the Rolls-Royce Trent powered Meteor took place here on 20th September 1945.

Although the airfield was reduced in use the base became a satellite to No 51 MU at Lichfield from August 1945 for the storage of aircraft and remained as such until 51 MU closed in July 1954. Although never a full operational station, it trained many Australian air crews, saw a few nickelling raids and played a fundamental part in the support of Bomber Command and the winning of the Second World War.

The airfield was quickly allowed to deteriorate as the buildings were of temporary war-time construction; but one B1 type hangar remains in civilian use and a few buildings remain scattered around the site. The land was held by the Ministry of Defence until 1975 and leased out. The airfield and surrounding dispersals and buildings were auctioned by Richardson & Linnell of Derby on 6 May 1975. The ten lots comprised the airfield as one, then still with complete runways, the other nine being a mix of buildings but including two hangars. Today there is very little to see at this once extremely busy satellite airfield, filled with Australian aircrew and responsible for the development of jet engines.

8

DARLEY MOOR

National Grid Reference SK175420, 3 miles S of Ashbourne, on the A515

Located literally on the A515, the main site is now bisected by the road so researchers will not have trouble finding this airfield. Another satellite airfield, Darley Moor was built with three concrete runways, one at 1,750 yards and two at 1,400 yards long, plus accommodation for 1,062 RAF and 183 WAAFs. Officially it opened in No 70 Group Army Support Command as the satellite to No 81 OTU at Ashbourne in July 1942, but the slow building progress hindered its opening operationally. Although officially the satellite to Ashbourne, the parent unit there did not receive any aircraft and the HQ moved to Whitchurch Heath in Shropshire in September 1942. Darley Moor was now ready for action and No 42 OTU arrived at Ashbourne on 26th October 1942, taking over this airfield as the satellite base for A Squadron with Ansons and Oxfords plus two Martinets and two Lysanders, later supplemented by Whitleys. As bad weather plagued both Darley Moor and Ashbourne, due to their high altitude, training progressed far too slowly to fulfil the urgent need for trained crews created by the pressure of war.

One parachuting demonstration took place in August 1943 to show how daylight parachuting operations are performed and another in October, when Master/Hotspur and Whitley/Horsa combinations took part. This coincided with the parent unit at Ashbourne being transferred to No 38 Group in November 1943 for airborne forces training now using Albemarle aircraft, which were designed as bombers but were woefully underpowered and relegated to training in multi-engine flying skills. Unfortunately

The one remaining crewroom at Darley Moor. (M. L. Giddings)

The remains of artwork inside the remaining hut at Darley Moor.
(M. L. Giddings)

they were so unreliable and inherently unstable when one engine failed that they were the cause of many deaths during the training process. Several accidents also occurred with the Whitleys. In the middle of July, one made a belly landing when it failed to gain any height. A few days later another Whitley came down in the sea after engine failure. Both crews were unhurt but very shaken. The third accident involving a Whitley at Darley Moor had more disastrous consequences when the entire crew lost their lives in the crash due to engine failure.

A prisoner of war episode (similar to von Werra at Hucknall – see Chapter 10) took place in January 1944, when an Italian attempted to steal an aircraft in his bid to get home. He was arrested and sent back to his PoW camp.

After intensive use of the Ansons and Oxfords, and later Albemarles, No 42 OTU was disbanded and absorbed into 81 OTU at Tilstock in March 1945. In preparation for that the Flight was withdrawn from Darley Moor and the airfield permanently closed on 18th February 1945. No 18 (P)AFU at Snitterfield planned to move to Ashbourne and Darley Moor in April 1945 but it was disbanded instead and the move never materialised.

Even though the airfield closed, the land and buildings remained for some time as No 28 MU at Buxton took the whole site over on 28th May 1945 for the storage of explosives and air ammunition, using both the runways and the hangars for maintenance. Darley Moor was one of several satellites used in this way during this period, with others at Ashbourne, Cairn Ryan, and Rowthorne Tunnel. This use continued until 23rd August 1954, when the RAF ensign was eventually and finally lowered to end the life of this base. Some of the dispersals are still visible but most buildings were quickly demolished and not very much remains to indicate that this was once an airfield, with a very intensive training role for our bomber pilots.

This building, now a private house, was originally the Link Trainer Unit at Darley Moor. (M. L. Giddings)

9

GAMSTON

National Grid Reference SK693762, 3 miles S of East Retford

Gamston was one of those airfields that were planned and built as standard bomber bases, but were never actually used as such. It had the usual three (hard) runway layout and the accommodation and technical buildings were as an operational bomber station yet it was used very little. One wonders if the site, once built, was thought to be unsafe in any way or did not allow for the fact that industrial smoke from Nottingham's factories would present a problem. Perhaps it is explained if we look at the method employed by the Air Ministry and the Works Directorate to designate sites to be airfields.

Initially it was just a case of looking at a 1-inch Ordnance Survey map to see which areas were free from obstructions within a 1,000 yard radius. The question of height above sea level also came into the picture with areas below 50 feet and above 650 feet being eliminated. Gamston obviously was found to be suitable for construction within these criteria and with Bomber Command demanding more and more bases, it became ready for use in December 1942. Despite the needs of the command, Gamston was deemed a satellite airfield for Ossington, where No 14(P)AFU were stationed with Airspeed Oxfords.

Not until May 1943 did the station become part of Bomber Command and then it came under the umbrella of No 93 Group, a training group. The arrival of 'C' Flight of No 82 OTU on 1st June, however, was to herald a new era. With Wellingtons and Martinets, they commenced a training routine that was to be used until October 1944.

At this juncture of the war, the OTUs were rarely asked to take part in major bombing operations. Unlike the earlier period, there were now enough bomber squadrons to carry the war back to the enemy. Most of the OTUs, including No 82, reverted to their primary role, that of training aircrew for four-engined aircraft. In addition to this, they had the Martinets on strength for gunnery training and also for affiliation training with Hurricanes. From June until August, the unit had an impressive accident-free record, for although several minor incidents occurred, there were no fatalities. This, considering the pace of training, says much for the instructors and their pupils. Many of the losses recorded subsequently, however, occurred through engine failure on the Wellingtons. With the bomber OTUs reaching their peak strength around late 1943, the demands on the aircraft became even greater. With this constant use, maintenance became more frequent and more efficient yet still the losses through engine failure continued. One incident concerning one of the Bristol Hercules XVIII engines that powered the Wellington X was when the port engine of HE201 lost power as it was climbing out of Gamston. This necessitated a crash landing but before this could be accomplished safely the aircraft hit trees five miles from Retford. Three of the crew, Fg Off J Coughlan DFM, Fg Off/H G Dayman RCAF and Plt Off J Christie RCAF, were, sadly, killed, with the other RCAF men, Fg Off H C McGavin, W/O R Tarling, Sgt J A S MacGregor and Sgt H D La Pointe, sustaining injuries.

A port engine failure was also the cause of a crash on the night of 22nd/23rd November 1943, when Wellington X LN601 came down at Norwell Woods House near Kneeshall Lodge. Having taken off from Desborough airfield at 21.58 hours, it was on a nickelling operation intending to drop leaflets in the St Nazaire region of France. Having climbed to 800 feet, the engine failed and the Wellington fell to earth. The explosion on impact with the ground killed the entire crew. When part of the aircraft was recovered by a salvage team, the inspection of the engine found evidence to suggest that a problem had caused the propeller to go into reverse pitch.

As we can tell from the few incidents mentioned, and there were many more, the pressures on trainees and instructors alike to absorb the complexities of flight, navigation, wireless procedures, gunnery and bomb aiming were immense. In line with all the OTUs, 82 saw its moments of triumph, but also more than its fair share of tragedies. The weeks before Christmas 1943 were almost trouble free but two days into the new year, six aircrew were lost when Wellington III BK387 crashed into high ground two miles SW of Keighley in Yorkshire when flying an evening navigation exercise from Ossington. W/O2 E I Glass, Fg Off J J McHenry, W/O2 J E Dalling, W/O2 J Henfrey, Sgt N W Crawford and Sgt E Savage were all members of the RCAF and were killed in the crash. Yet another bad incident occurred on the night of 3rd/4th February, when Wellington III HE749 took off from Gamston on a Bullseye (practice bombing) exercise. The last radio message was received at 23.22 hours, saying that it was returning to the airfield, but at 00.26 hours it dived into the ground at high speed. Striking the ground it instantly exploded, killing Sgt A C Fisher, Flt Sgt C D Jones RAAF, Sgt E H D Maguire RCAF, Sgt J L Barber RCAF and Sgt W R Waldron RCAF.

It is impossible within this book to record every accident and acknowledge the debt of every life. Suffice to say, each and every man who was killed or injured whilst flying from any of the OTUs, though not on operational flying, died in the service of his country.

In June 1944, a nucleus was taken from No 82 OTU to form No 86 OTU, which commenced a programme of training night bomber crews. Still equipped with the venerable Wellington, the unit continued to fly from Gamston with the consequence of further crashes, the first occurring when Wellington X HE821 left the airfield on a cross-country flight. At 800 feet it lost power, stalled and crashed at Henny Moor Farm, Creswell in Derbyshire. WO1 W D Murdie RCAF, Plt Off L M Brehaut RCAF, Fg Off/W W Cooper RCAF, Sgt J R Clarke RCAF and Sgt J J Lee RCAF were killed; all of them now rest in the Harrogate Cemetery.

As the last 12 months of war approached, Wg Cdr F F Rainsford DFC was appointed to command Gamston. This position usually demanded the rank of Group Captain but perhaps at this stage of the war, with victory in sight, it denoted the gradual rundown of the station. Yet, sadly, tragedy was still not far away. During the night of 30th August 1944 Wellington X HE485 left Gamston at 04.47 for a night exercise. Two minutes after lift-off it crashed at Haughton Hall, five miles from Retford, with the loss of all five RCAF aircrew. They too all rest in the

Gamston Christmas menu for 1944. (PRO Air 28/294)

Harrogate Cemetery. This was the second and last tragic accident to happen to the OTU before it disbanded on 15th October 1944.

Gamston was then transferred to No.7 Group Bomber Command and saw the arrival of No.3 Air Support from Shepherds Grove. This unit remained until January 1945, when flying again returned to Gamston in the form of No 30 OTU, again with Wellingtons. Transfer to No.91 Group took place on 12th June 1945 with the OTU disbanding at the same time. Gamston then became a major holding unit for RAAF aircrew awaiting repatriation to Australia until it finally closed in August 1945. Resurgence came during the Korean crises when, in May 1953, it opened as a satellite to Worksop, then the home of No 211 AFS flying jet Meteors and Vampires. They used Gamston continuously until final closure came in 1957. For a time part of the site was used by a civilian organisation operating a Dornier Skyservant, one of the newer civilian feeder aircraft. The airfield was kept viable by civilian companies and, in 1976, the RAF returned, using it again as a satellite, this time to No 6 FTS at Finningley, which used Gamston for its Bulldog trainers.

Gamston is now known as Retford and one runway (21/03, 1,203m long) remains for light aircraft, with a subsidiary runway used by the gliding school. Never a great RAF airfield, nevertheless, it is still in constant use as a small civilian airport.

10

HUCKNALL

National Grid Reference SK526470, 5 miles NNW of Nottingham

On the morning of 5th September 1940, the Luftwaffe launched an attack on Biggin Hill airfield in Kent. This was just one of many upon the airfield, a sector station in No 11 Group of Fighter Command. (See *Kent Airfields in the Second World War.*) There was also a feint attack against Croydon in an effort to draw up the British fighters and entice them away from Biggin Hill, which was the main target. The ruse failed as No 79 Squadron tore into the attack causing most of the bombs to fall short of the airfield.

The aircraft that had attacked Croydon were on their way home across Kent with an escort of Me109 fighters. Flying at the head of the second Gruppe of 109s was Hauptmann Erich von Selle. Immediately behind him flew two staff officers, Leutnant Heinrich Sanneman, technical officer, and Oberleutnant Franz von Werra, the adjutant. As they crossed the county they were attacked by Spitfires of No 41 Squadron from Hornchurch in Essex with the result that von Werra's aircraft was hit in the engine. As the bullets from Flt Lt John Webster's Spitfire struck it, his aircraft shuddered and lost height. Pulling the stick hard over, von Werra rolled to starboard to escape further hits but noticed that his Daimler Benz engine was not running as it should. Glancing at his instruments, he saw the temperature gauge shooting up. It was losing glycol and beginning to labour. Seconds later it spluttered, picked up and spluttered again, finally to stop altogether. Losing more height, more rapidly, von Werra looked for a flat area of land to attempt a crash landing. He saw an open field and pushed the stick forward. The 109 hit the ground heavily, bounced a few feet before coming back down and ploughing across a field of wheat stubble. It came to rest in a cloud of dust but did not catch fire.

Suddenly all was silent as von Werra opened his cockpit canopy and prepared to climb out. Pulling off his leather helmet, he jumped down to the ground and looked around him. Although not a sound was to be heard, his eyes caught a movement in the corner of the field. Several soldiers were climbing over a gate and running towards him. Should he run? Noticing they were armed, he thought better of it. As they approached, he pulled some personal papers from his top pocket and with a flick from his lighter, set fire to them. With guns raised the soldiers, who were from a local searchlight unit, approached von Werra, whereupon he decided to surrender himself to them.

He had crash-landed at Love's Farm, Winchet Hill, near Marden in Kent. Taken to Maidstone police station, he was interrogated and finally sent to Grizedale Hall Prisoner of War Camp in the Lake District. Determined to escape, his exploits were to bring him to one of the Nottinghamshire airfields,

The Me109 of von Werra which crashed at Marden in Kent on Thursday, 5th September 1940. (Kent Messenger)

Hucknall, from where he would make a determined attempt to steal an aircraft.

Hucknall airfield began life during the First World War, when the land was purchased from the Duke of Portland for a nominal sum. The contractors moved in and removed hedges and trees to construct a sizeable landing area, together with building hangars and technical and domestic buildings. It opened during 1917 as a training ground, a duty that it carried to the end of the First World War. On 1st March 1918, No 130 (Punjab) Squadron arrived with DeHavilland 9s, being joined the next month by No 135 Squadron. The latter saw no operational service before being disbanded on 4th July 1918, whilst No 130 carried out sorties before themselves being disbanded on the same date. No 205 arrived at Hucknall on 18th March 1918 flying the DH4 and the DH9, with No 218 (Gold Coast) Squadron arriving a month before. By the June of 1919, all the squadrons had been disbanded. The reason was that, with the armistice, the need for airfields became smaller, although it was hoped by many that Hucknall would remain. Considering that a considerable sum of money had been spent on its construction, it seemed a short-thinking policy to even consider closing it. However, with the end of 'the war to end all wars', killing machines and places of war were no longer required. The Government wanted to erase all memories of the conflict, including airfields. Hucknall did not survive and was put up for sale by the Air Ministry.

After the sale of one individual hangar and several dwellings, the 107-acre site was purchased by one George Elkington, a local farmer. It was fortunate that he did very little with the site, retaining the landing ground in its original state. Ironically, some time later the Air Ministry saw fit to purchase the site back from Mr Elkington, allowing the newly formed Nottingham Aero Club to use it. The Ministry also purchased further land around the airfield perimeter, but, finding the original site in a bad condition, began a re-building programme that was to take many months. The work was undertaken by John Laing, who brought the airfield and buildings up to the 1930s standard. This work included further brick-built technical and accommodation blocks. Upon completion, the airfield became earmarked for one of the Special Reserve Squadrons that were in the process of forming as the RAF gathered strength once again.

It fell to No 504 (County of Nottingham) Squadron to inaugurate the new lease of life for Hucknall. Formed on 26th March 1928 as a day bomber squadron, they were one of the Special Reserve Units that were the forerunners of the Auxiliary Air Force. Commanded by Sqn Ldr Edward Thornton, the squadron was equipped with the Hawker Horsley, one of the earliest post World War One biplane bombers. Initially of all wooden construction, the later models were of composite construction with the final marks being all metal. It was not produced in large numbers, the total eventually reaching 128. No 504 used the aircraft for six years and were in fact the last squadron to relinquish them. In 1935 the Horsley was replaced by an equally obsolescent biplane, the Westland Wallace. Produced as a private venture and a development of the Westland Wapiti, it was powered by a single Pegasus engine and could carry a 580lb bomb. Although very little improved from the Horsley, 504 Squadron put them to good use. They perfected a routine that earnt them the distinction of performing a dazzling display of precision flying in front of thousands of people at the 1934 RAF Hendon Display.

With the signs of another war forthcoming with Germany, all Special Reserve Units were embodied into the auxiliary air force on 18th May 1936. Originating from an idea first proposed by Sir

A pre-war photo of a Westland Wallace of No 504 (County of Nottingham) Auxiliary Squadron. (Bruce Robertson)

Hugh Trenchard in 1919, the auxiliary air force was not fully established until 1924. Only four squadrons were formed at that time, concerned solely with flying and pilot training. The rest remained Special Reserve Units until 1936. Squadrons were recruited by the County Territorial Army and Air Force Associations, with most of the members residing within their own county boundaries. Upnah House, on the corner of Forest Road, Nottingham, previously a girls' school, became the squadron headquarters. Embodiment into the air force proper was of great elation to all the members. At a gathering at Hucknall, the CO, Sqn Ldr H M Seely MP, read out a signal confirming the status amid much applause. Now they felt they were ready to get to grips with whatever was coming their way.

As if to mark their new role, in May 1937 the squadron received new aircraft in the shape of the Hawker Hind. Planned as an interim aircraft prior to the squadron's receiving the Battles and Blenheims, it was similar in a lot of details to the Hart but differed from the latter in being fitted with a super-charged Kestrel V engine and a tailwheel in place of a skid. It was the last biplane bomber to serve with the RAF, the last one leaving Bomber Command in 1938, but it continued to be used by the auxiliaries until the outbreak of war. With a top speed of 186mph at 16,400 feet, the pilots of 504 took no time in converting to them as the rumblings from Germany became all too obvious.

Hucknall, although grass, was a large airfield and quite capable of housing more than one squadron. With 504 taking the honour to be the first squadron to use the field, they were joined on 21st August 1936 by Nos 98 and 104 Squadrons. These were regular units in the air force, both equipped with the Hawker Hind. They carried out exercises with the auxiliary squadron until No 104 moved to Bassingbourn on 2nd May 1938 leaving No 98, now called 'Derby's Own', to begin its war at Hucknall equipped with the Fairey Battle single-engine monoplane bomber.

It was not only the military that were to use the airfield. As we see from the chapter on Rolls-Royce, in December 1934 they too moved into two of the large Belfast Truss hangars. It had become apparent by the early '30s that a large area of open space would be needed to further develop and test the aero engines. One employee of Rolls-Royce, Mr Cyril Lovesey, a private pilot with his own aircraft and a member of the Nottingham Flying Club, had seen the spare capacity at Hucknall and had proposed to the company the setting up of an operation there alongside the military. With formalities proceeding at a fast pace, Captain R Shepherd, of the same flying club, was appointed Chief Test Pilot. Initially there was a staff of fifteen, consisting of a maintenance team for the aircraft, an engineering team and administration personnel. The first aircraft to be used at the facility were a Hawker Hart, a Hawker Fury and a Gloster Gnatsnapper. With this scenario in place, work began on developing the engines. It was at Hucknall on 12th April 1935 that the PV12 engine flew for the first time installed in a Hart biplane. Upon its arrival at the Rolls-Royce facility, the first job was to perfect the cooling system. In the run-up to the beginning of the war, Hucknall was kept very busy indeed with the development and testing of the variant of this engine that finally was to power many aircraft – the Merlin.

Rolls-Royce's neighbours, No 504 Squadron had become a fighter squadron on 31st October 1938 equipped with the Gloster Gauntlet, the last of the RAF's biplane fighters. For them this was

The old 504 (County of Nottinghamshire) Squadron Belfast Truss hangars, still in good condition. (Author)

91

more or less a stop-gap aircraft pending the arrival of the new monoplane fighters. The new squadron crest incorporated an oak tree, known as the 'Major Oak Tree', fronted and eradicated and indicative of Sherwood Forest. Drawn from the armorial bearings of Nottingham County, it was considered an appropriate badge for a Hurricane squadron. The motto '*Vindicat in Venti*' (it avenges in the wind) was also indicative of the forest.

For 98 Squadron, it was continuation as a bomber squadron as they exchanged their ageing Hinds for another obsolescent aircraft, the Battle. No 1 Group established their headquarters at Hucknall and informed No 504 that they were to convert to the Hawker Hurricane. At last they were to receive the first of the new monoplane fighters but, disappointingly, were not to fly them in operations from Hucknall. A signal was received that the squadron was to move to Digby on 27th August 1939. Just before they moved, the squadron took part in the last Empire Air Day before the war. Held on 20th May 1939, it attracted an audience of over 32,000. The airfield was visited during the day by the Rt Hon Sir Kingsley Wood accompanied by the Chief of the Air Staff, Air Chief Marshal Sir Cyril Newall, GCB, CMG, CBE, the C-in-C Fighter Command, Air Chief Marshal Sir Hugh Dowding,

A Fairey Battle used as a testbed for the Merlin engine is seen outside the superb Belfast Truss hangar. (Rolls-Royce Heritage Trust)

GCVO, KCB, CMG and Air Vice Marshal J. L. Trafford Leigh-Mallory DSO.

Two months later, the Army Home Defence Scheme against air attack was put into place and orders were received for war markings to be painted on all aircraft. On 3rd September, the airfield lay within the area of No 12 Group Fighter Command with its headquarters at nearby Watnall. Commanded by Air Vice Marshal Trafford Leigh-Mallory, the underground operations room was just a mile from Hucknall airfield though, being Fighter Command, it had no responsibility for the airfield. Members of the Sherwood Foresters Regiment took up airfield defence duties and, much to the joy of the men, the first company of WAAFs arrived to take on clerical and other duties. On the eve of war, 98 Squadron commanded by Sqn Ldr J W Dixon-Wright, prepared itself. Some of the Battles had been detached to Weston Zoyland, Upwood and Bassingbourn. The broadcast by the Prime Minister, Neville Chamberlain, was relayed over the tannoy system. When he had finished, the base was hushed. Another broadcast by the squadron commanders followed, after which everyone was left to their own thoughts. All the wondering had finished. Hucknall was to go to war.

Although still within earshot of No 12 Group Fighter Command, no fighter squadrons were destined for the airfield. The day of 14th March 1940 did see a brief stay by a Polish training unit flying Battles but they had left by June. 98 Squadron left for Scampton on 2nd March and after brief stays at various airfields in the UK departed for Iceland in July, the first RAF aircraft to be despatched to the country in an effort to hit back at the enemy.

As the first phases of the Battle of Britain opened in the south, the airfield became a temporary headquarters for No 1 Group Bomber Command whilst No 1 (RAF) Ferry Pilots Pool led by Flt Lt G W H Wild formed to carry out the duties of ferrying repaired aircraft back to the squadrons. There formation was soon to become obvious as, depleted of any RAF squadrons, it was Rolls-Royce who really took the base to war. Their operation expanded rapidly with an increased test flying programme and the setting up of a section concerned with the repair of damaged Hurricanes. Once the repairs had been completed, it was the duty of the Ferry Flight to fly them back to the squadrons. On the further development of the Merlin, a new powerplant was designed and built at Hucknall for the Lancaster, as were the prototype installations for the Griffon engine on Beaufighter and Henley aircraft. During August and September 1940, the Hurricane repair line was kept busy. So much so that the unit contributed vital work in making sure the Hurricanes were repaired and returned to the squadrons as soon as possible. In order to retain a close contact with the military, Rolls-Royce formed an RAF Liaison Team. Its job was to inform and instruct the service on the operation of Rolls-Royce engines and to report back on problems being experienced. Many Hurricanes that came to Hucknall in a condition that can only be described as wrecks, came out of the workshops ready to fly another day.

As the Battle of Britain entered its fourth phase, von Werra had arrived at Officers' Camp No 1 Grizedale Hall in the Lake District towards the end of September 1940. Situated midway between Coniston Water and Windermere, the camp was in the middle of wild country. The house had been empty for a number of years until the War Office took it over and turned it into a POW camp. Within ten days of his arrival at Grizedale, von Werra had made his escape plans. On Monday 7th October, he and 23 other German officers set out on a route march from Grizedale, part of the normal exercise routine. Escorted by just a few British officers, he managed to give them the slip during a rest period. Dropping behind a wall, he crawled into long undergrowth and waited breathlessly. When the column once again moved off, he got up and ran in the opposite direction lest the guards suddenly realised he had gone. He made off towards a wood just as it began to rain.

And that is how it was; it rained for the next five days and nights. Back at Grizedale the alarm had been raised and a full search was put into operation. Lorries, cars and motorcycles sped off into the wet night to look for him, but von Werra had vanished. On 12th October, the sixth day of his escape, the military began searching the woods into which he had fled. They were joined by members of the Cumberland and Westmorland Constabulary who, during a break for refreshment, were told by a local sheep farmer that a man had been seen on a hill about a half mile away. All thoughts of refreshment vanished as the searchers made for the spot. The ground became soft and boggy as they got higher but, noticing a slight movement among some tufts of grass situated in a very wet area, they ran forward.

Immediately one of the searchers sank into the boggy surface only to find von Werra lying on his back sunk into the bog with just his face above it. Dragging him out, he was handcuffed and once again marched into captivity. Taken back to Grizedale and interrogation, he had his last sight of the Hall as he was ordered to be taken to a new camp.

This time it was POW (Officers') Transit Camp No 13 near Swanwick, Derby. It was a converted country house called The Hayes lying about half a mile from Swanwick village. After several more interviews, von Werra was shown to his room and was amazed to find that many of his fellow officers were also at Swanwick. Within a few days his thoughts were once again turning to escape, this time in collaboration with the other Luftwaffe officers. It was decided that a tunnel was the best bet, one of which was started on 17th November 1940. Over the following weeks the tunnel grew in length despite many difficulties such as dispersal of earth and ventilation. It had been decided that the initial breakout should be made by five men, including von Werra. He was to take the identity of a Dutch pilot of a crashed Wellington bomber belonging to a 'special squadron'. He would use the name 'Captain van Lott' and say that he had flown from Dyce in Scotland, an RAF base that he had read about in English papers and the one that was the furthest distance from Swanwick. It was his intention, once he had got through the tunnel, to make for the nearest airfield in the hope of stealing a plane and flying back to Germany.

The tunnel was completed by the 17th December, one month after it was begun. Three days later, five men entered it just as the Air Raid sirens began to wail around the area. After what seemed like an eternity, a hole was pushed up through the frosty ground and fresh air hit the escapees. As they emerged an air raid was in full swing on nearby Derby. This was, of course, the perfect cover as all the lights in the camp had been switched off. Shaking hands with his fellow officers, von Werra made for the outskirts of a wood close by. The 'all clear' sounded in the Notts/Derby area at around 4.30 am. Hearing the hiss of steam coming from a nearby railway siding, von Werra walked towards a train that was awaiting its freight wagons. Explaining to a shunter that he was a Dutchman serving with the RAF, he was taken along the track towards the station. Reaching Codnor Park station at around 5.30 am, the shunter handed him over to the signalman/clerk, Mr R

Oberleutnant Franz von Werra. He was the adjutant of No 2 Gruppe, 3rd Fighter Geschwader.

W Harris. After hearing von Werra's explanation of his situation, much to the consternation of the German, Mr Harris suggested that he wait for the booking clerk to come on duty in order that he (Mr Harris) could ring the military from the GPO telephone in the booking office. The wait for the clerk to arrive was considerable and all the time von Werra was thinking how he could continue his bluff. When the clerk did finally arrive, von Werra asked him which was the nearest RAF station and was told that it was Hucknall, about 10 miles away. Von Werra then suggested that the clerk should ring the base and ask for transport to come and pick him, von Werra, up. Sam Eaton, the ticket clerk, first rang the local police, who arrived quickly in the form of several plain-clothes officers. Managing to convince them that his story was true, von Werra inwardly sighed with relief and again insisted that the clerk contact Hucknall. This Sam Eaton did and spoke to the Duty Officer, who arranged for a car to be sent. Sure that his plan was working, von Werra was transported to Hucknall airfield.

Upon his arrival he was subjected to several interviews in the Adjutant's office as the duty personnel became suspicious. He was introduced to Sqn Ldr Boniface, the Duty Officer, who, after questioning him further, attempted to ring Dyce airfield to enquire about 'Captain van Lott'. Von Werra made an excuse to use the toilet and taking this opportunity to escape he ran from the office towards the Rolls-Royce hangars. Once out in the open and now in daylight he could see that none of the aircraft in view were suitable for him to make his escape. He continued walking and found himself approaching the Rolls-Royce site, which had several Hurricanes outside that had been repaired or modified. He stopped and spoke to a group standing beside one of them and, following a conversation with a watchman, was taken to the dispersal office. Here he passed himself off as a ferry pilot who had come to collect a Hurricane. He was believed, it not being unusual for ferry pilots to be foreigners who had escaped to Britain.

Von Werra confessed that he was not familiar with the Hurricane's controls and was then taken to an aircraft, where they were explained to him. Whilst all this was taking place, there had been a telephone conversation between the office and the RAF station headquarters, who by now were looking for von Werra. It was quickly realised that he was now with Rolls-Royce and a detachment of soldiers, led by an RAF Officer, was sent to

Station Commander at Hucknall, Gp/Cpt Hughes-Chamberlain (right) and Sqn/Ldr Boniface, Duty Officer, at the time of the von Werra incident.

arrest him. They found him seated in the Hurricane, whereby the officer climbed onto the wing and, pointing a revolver at von Werra, told him to get out.

So near and yet so far. Clambering out of the cockpit, he was taken under armed escort to the guard room. Within two weeks he was on his way to Canada, escaping whilst in transit and eventually, via the USA, Mexico and South America, reaching Germany. He was the first and only German POW in British hands to do so.

The station diarist recorded the event sparingly: '21.12.40. Escaped German prisoner attempted to pass himself off as a Dutch pilot of Coastal Command and tried to commandeer a Hurricane'. The official report to the Air Ministry did little more.

Upon his arrival in Berlin Franz von Werra was awarded a Knight's Cross from the hands of Adolf Hitler himself. Ten months later he was dead, killed in an un-explained flying accident off the Dutch coast. For Hucknall, however, the incident was one of the more unusual aspects of its war. (A full account of von Werra's escapades is given in the book *The One That Got Away*, by Kensal Burt and James Leasor. Franz von Werra was also the subject of a Rank film of the same title.)

When all the excitement had died down, Hucknall returned to its normal status of a training and repair airfield. Defence had now been given over to the RAF with the Sherwood Foresters Battalion moving to a different theatre of the war. Christmas 1940 saw very little flying with the exception of Rolls-Royce test flights. However, January 1941 saw the return of Polish airmen when No 1 (Polish) Flying Training School formed at the airfield with a selection of Tiger Moths, Battles and twin-engined Oxfords. They arrived at a time of significant snowfall, allowing the station snow clearing plan to be put into operation. This entailed all trainees being issued with shovels and brooms to clear the landing area and the pathways. Being used to harsh weather, the snow clearing did not deter the Poles at all. Re-designated No 16 (Polish) SFTS in June, it moved to Newton the

A Tiger Moth of No 25 (Polish) EFTS. Note the Polish emblem on the side. (David Birch)

following month to be replaced by another Polish unit, No 25 (Polish) EFTS. Arriving from Peterborough on 16th July 1941, they were to continue flying from Hucknall for the rest of the war.

Over on the other side of the airfield, Rolls-Royce had been expanding to accommodate the increase in damaged aircraft. Development of the Merlin engine had reached what became known as the Merlin 65. This engine was installed in a North American Mustang and was flown on test flights within three months. These experiments ultimately led to the production of the Merlin engined P.51 Mustang, which had the Packard V-1650 American made version of the Merlin installed. Earlier the same engineers were converting Spitfire Vs to Spitfire IXs in order to counter the new German FW190. There is no doubt that the development work carried out at Hucknall made a significant contribution to the Merlin engine's performance.

The Polish airmen were now flying many long hours, indicated by the fact that in February 1941, the total flying hours were 826 hours 10 minutes. They had been spurred on by the news that their Commander-in-Chief, General Wladyslaw Sikorski, had negotiated with the Air Ministry for all Polish airmen to cease to be members of the Royal Air Force Volunteer Reserve and in future be part of the Polish Air Force. This would remain subject to the RAF in many matters, including, training, discipline and operations, but would have its own Polish identity. The Polish airmen regarded General Sikorski as more than just a commander. He had led them since they had been forced to flee their homeland and he had guided them through the traumas of flying from France and their arrival in Britain. It came as a tragic shock to all of them when, on 5th July 1943, the plane carrying him back to London from the Middle East crashed into the sea shortly after taking off from Gibraltar. There were no survivors and every Polish man and woman lost a father figure. The effect of this tragedy was felt throughout all the personnel at Hucknall. Sikorski had been his country's equal to Churchill and he would be sorely missed.

Tragedy returned to Hucknall when, on 20th April 1941, Tiger Moth N6916 was taking off on a cross country flight. As the Moth ran down the grass runway, a Battle that was landing at the same time collided with it, killing both crews. Incidents like this were all too common with limited airfield control and the fact that most of the flying was being done by trainees. Better weather

The Polish Training Camp still standing in good condition in 2002. (Author)

allowed the flying hours to increase, with June showing that 2,011 hours 20 minutes had been achieved, though an increase in accidents was also recorded.

Training continued throughout 1942. So intense did it become that a Relief Landing Ground was opened at Papplewick Moor. This was not an easy airfield for student pilots to negotiate owing to several problems with the land. Thus they were warned to carry out approaches only and not land.

Although a very busy airfield, Hucknall was still only grass. With the rapid advances in jet propulsion and the fact that Rolls-Royce were now designing and building the Whittle jet, it was impossible to test fly jet aircraft from grass. Balderton, which by now had hard runways, was initially chosen for testing and arrangements were made to move part of the test facility. However, within months a more permanent base had been found at Church Broughton.

Very little changed at Hucknall to interfere with the day to day training routine. With a change in Air Ministry policy and the formation of the Air Defence of Great Britain Command, No 12 Group Communications Flight moved in to remain there until peacetime, responsible for flying the high ranking officers of this Fighter Command HQ. On 17th January 1945, the Poles heard that Warsaw had been liberated by Polish troops. The celebrations at Hucknall ran through into the night and well into the next day. By March, the city of Cologne had fallen and American troops had moved into Bonn. Despite these signs of the end of conflict, training continued as hard as ever. Only after the VE Day celebrations was the pace allowed to slacken.

Peacetime brought No 504 (County of Nottingham) Squadron, R.AuxAF back to its home base. It reformed as a light bomber unit in May 1946 but the following year became a night-fighter squadron flying the DeHavilland Mosquito NF30. In May 1948 it reverted to a day fighter squadron and converted to Spitfire F.22s before moving to Wymeswold. The Nottingham University Air Squadron was re-instated at the airfield and joined by No 664 Squadron of the R.AuxAF flying the little Auster V. A maintenance unit was finally based there but with the

Hucknall viewed post-war and virtually unchanged. The Rolls-Royce factory is centre front, with the Polish Training Camp behind it and the main RAF site alongside the Belfast Truss hangars. Several test aircraft can be seen outside, including a Lancaster and a Canberra. (Rolls-Royce Heritage Trust)

disbandment of all the auxiliary squadrons in March 1957, Hucknall was left with Rolls-Royce. This facility continues today, with Hucknall being classified as a private airfield operated, appropriately, by the Merlin Flying Club. With the von Werra episode, the airfield was assured of a place in the history books. One wonders what repercussions would have taken place had he succeeded in his daring escapade. It was a very close thing!

11

LANGAR

National Grid Reference SK740335, 10 miles SE of Nottingham

During the First World War, experiments were carried out to develop a system of runway lighting. Initially, Goose Neck flares were used – large metal jug-type canisters containing paraffin and a wick. Since this method entailed airmen lighting and placing them along the runway, thus taking a long time, the next idea was to place several, electrically controlled lights on a pole, therefore lighting a large area and being quick to switch on and off should the enemy appear overhead. It was, however, the growth of civil aviation during the 1920s that accelerated the idea of safe runway and airfield lighting. With further progress, taxi-track lighting was introduced to enable pilots to see their way off the runway and to the dispersal areas. One Nottinghamshire airfield played a part in the latter experiments, the result of which culminated in the modern airport lighting systems we have today.

Situated between the villages of Langar and Harby, 10 miles SE of Nottingham, Langar, though intended as a main bomber base, saw only one squadron in residence throughout the war. With construction work starting in March 1940, it had the usual three runway layout. Building continued throughout the year and into 1941, the site finally opening in 1942 under the umbrella of No 5 Group, Bomber Command. Langar was not only a military base as, in September 1942, the aircraft manufacturers A V Roe and Co Ltd opened a workshop facility on the west side of the airfield. This was built for the servicing and re-conditioning of the

The prototype Avro Lancaster III, now fitted with Rolls-Royce Merlin engines. (MAP)

Lancaster bomber, perhaps the most famous bomber of the war.

With its completion, Langar prepared to receive its first and only operational squadron, No 207. They arrived on 20th September 1942 from nearby Bottesford, having converted from the ill-fated Avro Manchester and Handley Page Hampden to the Mk I Lancaster. Commanded by Wg Cdr Jeffs, No 207 was the third squadron to commence working on the type at this early phase of the war. Previously they had had the dubious task of pioneering the Manchester into service. This had not been a happy time for the squadron owing to the engine problems that had occurred with the type. The Manchester had proved to be one of the great disappointments of the Second World War, with its failure on operations and its unpopularity with the crews that flew it. It had first entered operational service with 207 Squadron at Waddington in November 1940, with the first raid taking place on the night of 24th/25th February 1941, when Brest was the target. Now they were happy to be converting to the Lancaster with high hopes.

By the time the squadron reached Langar, they had suffered several losses. With flying training beginning on 15th March 1942, fifteen days later the first Lancaster was lost in tragic

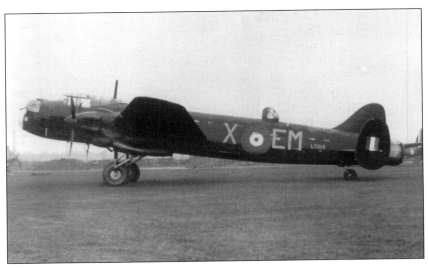

A 207 Squadron Avro Manchester, pictured at Langar. The forerunner of the Lancaster, it did not live up to expectations. (RAF Museum P6299)

circumstances over Lincolnshire. The accident happened when Sergeant N A Lingard, flying Lancaster R5501/EM, was carrying out a practice flight in the vicinity of Lincoln. Unbeknown to him, a Miles Master, DK973, was carrying out a similar flight within the same airspace. The pilot of the Master suddenly saw the Lancaster and, for some reason, attempted a mock attack on it. In doing so, he mis-judged his distance and collided with the tail of the bomber. Both aircraft went out of control and crashed, with the Lancaster of 207 Squadron hitting the ground east of Bracebridge. Sadly there were no survivors.

The second incident took place on 7th/8th of April. A Lancaster being flown by Flt Sgt J McCarthy suddenly lost the two starboard engines and crashed on the boundary of Bottesford airfield. Miraculously, both he and the rest of the crew emerged unscathed whilst the aircraft was destroyed. It was not a good time for 207 Squadron. In just three months, eight aircraft had been written off in accidents, yet it must be said that at this period the Lancaster was relatively untested and the crews unskilled in operating large, four-engined bombers.

Once the squadron had settled into Langar and the working-up period had passed, operational flying began. The first operation from Langar took place on 23rd September, the target being Wismar. The main targets over the coming months would be Bremen, Essen, Cologne and Dusseldorf amongst many others, and with the increase in operations, inevitably, the losses mounted. During May, June, July and August, the squadron lost several crews whilst flying from Bottesford. The first major incident whilst flying from Langar happened on 24th October, when Lancaster W4121/EM-B, flown by Flg Sgt L R Wright was part of a force attacking Milan. On the return flight, sadly, the Lancaster crashed into the sea off Blainville sur Mer (Manche), France with the loss of all the crew.

In the early hours of 8th November, Operation 'Torch', the allied landings at Algiers, Oran and Casablanca, took place. As a preliminary softening up, 175 bombers, including Lancasters from 207 Squadron, had raided Genoa. Having showered the port with high explosive and incendiaries, four aircraft were lost on the return journey, including one aircraft, Lancaster L7546/EM-G from 207 Squadron, flown by Plt Off R S Wilson. A similar incident occurred on 25th November, when Lancasters carried out a raid on Bad Zwischemahn. Whilst the raid was a success, Flt Lt R J Hannan DFC crashed near Eaton in Lincolnshire in Lancaster R5694/EM-F, so near to home. Return sorties to Turin on 9th December brought tragedy to Lancaster R5570/EM-R when Wg Cdr F G L Bain failed to return. December 1942 was to prove the worst regarding Lancaster crashes with many squadrons losing aircraft and good crews.

It was not only on operations that aircraft were lost. During the working up period on the type the OTUs had their fair share of tragedy. For 207, the month ended on a sad note when Sgt J R Walker and his crew in Lancaster W4191/EM-Q crashed near Elst in the Netherlands on 22nd December.

Christmas was somehow celebrated in the usual style at Langar but an air of sadness about the losses still cast a shadow over the proceedings. Bad weather prevented flying over the New Year period but spring 1943 saw the squadron carry out sorties as far afield as Poland and the toe of Italy. The crest of the squadron showed a 'Winged Lion Statent' with the motto 'Semper Paratus' (Always Prepared), this being very apt for a squadron that was at the forefront of Arthur Harris's bombing campaign.

By now the war was beginning to move at an increased tempo as the United States 8th Air Force made its first raid on Germany.

The memorial to 207 Squadron stands at the main entrance to Langar airfield, the motto 'Always Prepared'. (Author)

With that event taking place on 27th January 1943, the 4th February saw the 8th Army enter Tunisia. Plans were being formulated for an invasion of the European mainland by seaborne and airborne troops. The latter would require gliders to be towed by tug aircraft and, like many airfields within the area, Langar was to be used to store the Airspeed Horsa gliders. With 207 Squadron continuing to play its part in the bombing offensive over Germany, space at the airfield became premium. The squadron was now replacing its Mk I Lancasters with the Mk III, the only difference being that the engines were now licence-built American Packard Merlins. (See the chapter on Rolls-Royce.) In addition the aircraft were fitted with the Martin 250-CE23 electrically driven, mid-upper turret with 0.5 inch guns. By this time the Mk III was being built in Canada by Victory Aircraft of Toronto, which eventually delivered 430 examples of the Lancaster.

A very important raid took place on 17th August, when the squadron was detailed to be part of a force to attack the secret experimental rocket site at Peenemunde. In all, 597 aircraft of Bomber Command were in the air at the same time with No 207 being the last squadron to bomb. The attack was carried out from 5,000 feet in full moonlight with the target in full view. The squadrons had not been told just what Peenemunde was but it was made perfectly clear at the briefing that it was an important target and that if it was missed, the operation would be on again night after night until it was hit. This did not happen and all of 207's Lancasters returned safely to Langar content that a job had been well done.

On the night of 3rd/4th of September 1943, 207 were briefed to attack Berlin. This was a high profile raid and it was arranged that the BBC correspondent Wynford Vaughan-Thomas and his sound engineer, Reg Pidsley, would fly in Lancaster ED586 F-Freddie and record the entire raid from take-off to landing back at Langar. Vaughan-Thomas was told to describe exactly what went on and what he saw with no window dressing. After the afternoon test flight and a briefing, the raid was deemed 'on'. There was certainly no window dressing as the operation was recorded faithfully for transmission over the wireless later. The outbound trip, the bombing of the target and even an encounter with an enemy nightfighter which was shot down by one of the gunners increased the tension in Vaughan-Thomas's voice. The last few minutes of the recording give an indication of his relief and the crews sense of achievement: "We came home as the dawn broke clear and calm. We received our signal to land and that gentle bump on the tarmac was the sweetest sound I ever heard. It didn't seem to matter that another Lancaster had landed on the wrong runway and went across our bows. We were down intact. I didn't exactly kiss the ground as we got into the truck to go to the de-briefing, but I felt like doing it. The pilot grinned and said, 'I was right, wasn't I? I told you you'd enjoy it.'

With the Americans now fully committed to the war they needed bases on UK soil, and Langar was earmarked to become one of them. On 12th October 1943, No 207 Squadron moved over to Spilsby. For over a year they had flown from Langar and whilst they had seen tragedy with the loss of 247 aircrew, they had also seen success in the bombing campaign. Now they were to continue the struggle from a new base.

The airfield went into a hectic stage whilst preparations were made to receive the Americans. These were hurriedly achieved and on 30th October, No 10 Service Group and the 27th Mobile Repair and Reclamation Squadrons arrived. With the service units in place, the 435th Troop Carrier Group arrived at Langar on 3rd November. Constituted in America on 30th January and activated on 25th February 1943, they equipped with Douglas C-47s (Dakota to the British) and C-53s in preparation for duty overseas with the 9th Air Force. They arrived at Langar direct from Baer Field, Indiana and went straight into a period of intense training for participation in the airborne operation.

Langar was now Army Air Force Station 490 as many training exercises began. One in particular, code-named Operation 'Eagle', was a paratroop drop at night. As dusk fell, the troops embarked on the C-47s. The roar of Pratt and Witney engines filled the air as the aircraft got airborne. Over the county of Nottinghamshire, people in the streets looked up as the armada flew overhead, never suspecting that this was a practice for the greatest invasion in history. All aircraft returned safely after a successful drop. A second exercise was with British troops. Again it was a night drop near Winterbourne Stoke on Salisbury Plain and once again the C-47s dropped paratroops directly on the zone indicated. However, the 435th TCG were not to take part in 'Overlord' whilst at Langar and on 25th January 1944 they moved to Welford (Wiltshire), Station No 474, under the command of Colonel Frank J MacNees. They were replaced by the 441st TCG, again equipped with C-47s and C-53s. They also began an intense routine of practice paratroop drops by day and by night but again, were not to fly from Langar for the landings. They departed to Merryfield (Somerset) on 25th April, leaving the airfield devoid of any aircraft.

Langar did not go into Care and Maintenance, but was used as a store and a place to build the American Waco Hadrian Gliders. Designed by the Waco Aircraft Company of Troy, Ohio, the Hadrian first received the designation CG-4a for the USAAF. The type was first supplied to the RAF in 1943 and made its mark during the invasion of Sicily in July 1943. Unlike British gliders, which were all wooden, the Hadrian had a steel tubular fuselage. It carried a crew of two and could transport thirteen troops plus a light cargo, which was placed in the glider via a nose section that hinged upwards just aft of the crew compartment. Apart from the landings at Sicily, they were not used by the RAF but found plenty of use by the Americans. The aircraft were shipped to Langar in parts and re-assembled in the hangars in preparation for the landings. This work took place until May 1944, by which time over 200 had been issued to the troop carrying groups.

Langar played no part in Operation 'Overlord', the invasion of mainland Europe. It had been planned to hand the station back to the RAF in July but this was delayed due to the Americans still needing bases after D-Day. August saw the station languish, which came as an anti-climax to the personnel stationed there. However, with D-Day over, September saw a resurgence of use as the plans for Operation 'Market Garden' became known. Langar returned to the USAAF and back came the 441st TCG.

History records 'Market Garden' as one of the 'if only's' of the war. Its failure was the air plan, which had been devised by the Air Staff. All three airborne divisions suffered because the landings were in daylight, the intended drop zones were too far from the objective and lack of aircraft meant that the troop drops had to be carried out over three days. This cost the operation the element of surprise. At Arnhem the lack of close air support enabled the enemy to bring in heavy reinforcements. This placed the 1st Airborne Division in a desperate position for, without this support, ie fighter and bomber, the enemy became over-whelming. The glory of 'Market Garden' belonged to the un-armed transport aircraft which carried the airborne troops. Theirs was a job well done despite the misfortunes of the

The Langar ORB entry for the arrival of the US 9th Troop Carrier Command. (PRO-Air 28/440)

planning. Included in this appraisal were, of course, the Americans flying from Langar.

On 17th September, 45 C-47s took off for Drop Zone 'T', west of Nijmegen. They carried 1,922 paratroopers coloquially called the 'Screaming Eagles'. The outbound flight was uneventful and a good drop was made. This, however, was the only sortie that 441st TCG were to cover as they returned to Merryfield directly after leaving. Langar was once again under Care and Maintenance.

The usual course for a would-be bomber pilot to follow was flying training at an OTU, usually on twin-engined aircraft, and then to be passed out to go to an operational squadron flying similar aircraft. Due to the fact that most of the bomber squadrons were now flying four-engined aircraft, another stage of training was required between the OTU and operations. The establishment of the heavy conversion units filled this gap, with one of them, No 1669 HCU, being formed at Langar on 15th August 1944. Not until the Americans left, however, did the aircraft arrive in the form of Halifax and Lancasters and a few

A post-war Canadian invitation to a cocktail party at RCAF Langar.
(Notts Library)

Hurricanes and Spitfires for fighter co-operation and inter-
ception practice. Once again the sound of heavy aircraft graced
Langar, but with the war in its final months, No 1669 HCU
disbanded on 16th March 1945.

Avro, meanwhile, on the other side of the airfield, had
continued their war repair work admirably. With very little
attention from enemy aircraft, the organisation had carried out
sterling work. Even though the war was reaching its end, the unit
continued at Langar finally to relinquish the workshops and
hangars in September 1968. For the rest of the airfield, with the
disbanding of the HCU, it was back to Care and Maintenance.
Part of the site was handed over briefly to the Ministry of Aircraft
Production, but on 15th December 1946, except for the airfield
the base closed completely, with the exception of the Avro works.
All military personnel were posted away and Langar's military
buildings were left to decay for five years.

A new lease of life came in 1951 when the site was surveyed
and found suitable for a base for the Royal Canadian Air Force,

Langar Control Tower on a damp afternoon in 2002. The British Parachute School was determined to continue. (Author)

then, as now, part of the NATO Alliance Organisation. Langar now came under the control of No 1 Air Division with its HQ at Metz in France. This necessitated a large building programme, much of it the provision of new living quarters for the personnel. Frequent aircraft movements consisted of Bristol Freighters and Beechcraft Expeditors, although the main purpose of the establishment was to contain and issue spare parts for aircraft of the RCAF. The Canadians became a familiar sight in Nottingham and the surrounding area and such was their welcome by the people of the county that a maple tree was planted at Langar, presented by the people of Gransby in Quebec. They remained for eleven years but, with changes in NATO policy, left in 1963.

A V Roe, which had continued working throughout, stayed until September 1968. With their departure, Langar closed for the last time. It did not sink entirely into obscurity and today is operated by British Parachute Schools. Two shortened runways remain in use and some of the wartime buildings remain. Though never finding fame and glory, Langar certainly played its part in winning the war, and to commemorate this fact a memorial to all who gave their lives was erected at the wartime entrance.

12

NEWTON

National Grid Reference TL915426, 7 miles E of Nottingham

In 1938, a voluntary organisation for young men interested in aviation was formed. Known as the Air Defence Cadet Force (ADCF), it was created by the Air League of the British Empire under the direction of Air Commodore J A Chamier, CB, CMG, DSO, OBE. Such was the interest that units were formed in cities, towns and even schools. Cadets were encouraged to visit airfields and assist the groundcrews, a task that continued all through the Battle of Britain and beyond. On 1st February 1941, the then Secretary of State for Air, Sir Archibald Sinclair, changed the name to the Air Training Corps and broadcast an appeal to the nation's youth to join the new organisation. At the end of the war, a new RAF command was formed. Known as the RAF Reserve Command, it re-created and encompassed the Auxiliary Air Force, the University Air Squadrons and the Air Training Corps. The command ran from 1946 until 1950, when the name changed to Home Command. In 1959, it came under the control of Flying Training Command. In 1960, the Corps was given its own status, Headquarters Air Cadets, and in 1975 it was established at one of the most well known grass airfields in Nottinghamshire, RAF Newton.

Situated 7 miles east of the city, Newton was one of the airfields established during the expansion period. It was one of the last permanent stations to be constructed before war broke out, but was not fully utilised until July 1940. Part of No 1 Group, it was quickly put to use with the arrival of Nos 103 and 150

The De Havilland Chipmunk was used at Newton to give Air Cadets air experience. (MAP)

Squadrons. Both had been part of the Advanced Air Striking Force in France, but had been forced to retreat as the Germans advanced towards the Channel coast. With both squadrons flying the Fairey Battle light bomber, No 103 had left Souge in a hurry on 14th June whilst No 150 had left Pouan in a similar fashion at the same time.

The Fairey Battle was one of the types chosen by the Air Ministry for the expanding pre-war RAF. The first of the monoplane bombers, it carried twice the bomb load of the biplane Harts and Hinds twice as far. It held out great hope for the future bombing strategy, but, in the event, with its single 1,030hp Rolls-Royce Merlin engine, proved to be underpowered. The same was proved with the armament of a single Browning machine-gun firing forward and one Vickers 'K' gun aft, fitted at the rear of the cockpit. An indication of the aircraft's failure can be gained by the fact that on 30th September 1939, during an unescorted daylight reconnaissance operation over the Saar, four out of five Battles of 150 Squadron were shot down by Messerschmitt fighters. Heavily depleted, all the Battle squadrons returned to the UK and became part of No 1 Group Bomber Command, being based at Binbrook in Lincolnshire and at Newton.

Hawker Hunter Mark 1 Gate guardian at RAF Newton. (P. Grundy)

Once the squadrons had settled into their new base, the squadron commanders, Wg Cdr T C Dickens of 103 and Wg Cdr Hesketh DFC of 150, were told that due to the condition of the Battles they had flown from France, replacement aircraft would be arriving shortly. When they did so, the squadrons would be required to carry out attacks on the enemy-held French ports. Intelligence and reconnaissance had shown that the Germans were preparing for a sea and air assault on the British mainland. The photos had shown large concentrations of barges waiting in the ports for the right weather and the right time to cross the Channel. Soon after the new aircraft had arrived, the squadrons commenced bombing attacks on Calais and Boulogne in conjunction with other bomber and army co-operation squadrons. Mainly carried out at night owing to the vulnerability of the aircraft, there were losses nevertheless, though not on the scale previously experienced. Aircraft recognition (or lack thereof) was to blame for one incident, in which a Bristol Blenheim nightfighter on patrol mis-identified and shot down one of the Battles.

Re-equipment of all No 1 Group aircraft meant that the Battles were withdrawn from frontline service with Bomber Command in October 1940. Their replacement was the Vickers Wellington

IC, more commonly known as the 'Wimpey'. This was a great advance on the Battles and both squadrons took to it readily. Designed to Air Ministry Spec B.9/32 issued in September 1932, the prototype Wellington (K4049) made its maiden flight on 15th June 1936. Incorporating the Barnes Wallis geodetic method of construction, the aircraft was able to take a lot of punishment. More than two and a half thousand of the IC were built, this being the most common variant during the early days of the war. No 103 Squadron were to receive the IC whilst No 150 received the IC and the IA.

After a very brief conversion period, the Wellingtons were soon continuing the bombing of enemy harbours. By October, the threat of a German invasion, code-named 'Sealion', had receded somewhat due to the failure of Goering's Luftwaffe in clearing the skies of Fighter Command above the south eastern corner of the UK. The follow-up bombing operations were to ensure that 'Sealion' would never take place. By this time, however, a new threat had appeared in the shape of the German Navy, which was attacking our capital ships and convoys.

At 7 am on 22nd March 1941, two of Germany's 32,000-ton

The Vickers Wellington was the early aircraft used by most Polish bomber squadrons. This photo shows 311 (Czech) Sqdn. (Crown)

battleships, the Scharnhorst and the Gneisenau, had slipped quietly into Brest harbour and tied up. Both were in need of major repairs and the progress of these was monitored secretly by the French Resistance, who passed the information to London. For eight days after the ships' arrival, the weather was against any flying operations from the UK, but on the evening of 30th March the skies cleared and the air-raid sirens sounded around the dockyard of Brest. As they did so, a force of Wellington bombers, including Nos 105 and 150 Squadrons, attacked the ships. The target for the two Newton-based units was the Gneisenau. Five-hundred pound armour-piercing bombs rained down upon the dockyard. In a matter of seconds, fire and devastation had taken hold as many of the bombs missed the Gneisenau and instead hit a building lying some distance back from the quay. This was a hotel full of German naval officers, many of whom perished in the ensuing fire. Unfortunately, not one of the bombs dropped hit the ship. However, when the fires had died down, German marine experts found fragments of the armour-piercing bombs and then knew that the RAF were now out to sink the ships come what may. In this instance, their intelligence was right, for, several days after this initial attack, Coastal Command and Bomber Command mounted raids on the dockyard. Gneisenau was eventually hit by a Coastal Command Beaufort torpedo attack, resulting in a six months' repair. Although the Wellingtons of the Newton-based squadrons did not hit the main target, all aircraft returned safely, content that they were at least the forerunners of further major attacks on Germany's navy.

The year continued in similar vein with both squadrons carrying out further raids over Germany and the low countries. In July, a signal was received at Newton stating that the base was to be transferred from Bomber Command to Flying Training Command with immediate effect. Though this news did not please the Wellington squadrons, who had come to look upon Newton as home over the past year, a safe airfield was needed for Polish airmen undergoing flying training. On 11th July 1941, No l03 left for Elsham Wolds with No 150 leaving a day earlier for Snaith and conversion to the Wellington III. Newton was about to enter a very different phase.

At the outbreak of war in 1939, the Polish Air Force had twelve fighter squadrons. The pilots were well trained and during

September 1939, had destroyed 126 German aircraft with a loss of 114 of their own. Following the Russian invasion of Poland on 17th September, many of the Polish pilots escaped via Rumania, Hungary and Italy to France, where they joined the French Air Force in the hope of carrying on the fight. When France fell, over 5,500 came to Britain, where they re-formed as an independent air force under British command. There were no military bands to welcome them, no reception committee. They were just given a cup of tea, sandwiches and put on a train to Eastchurch airfield in Kent. By early 1940, two Polish squadrons with 154 pilots were preparing to take part in the Battle of Britain and by March 1941, the Polish squadrons amounted to one eighth of the strength of Fighter Command. Four Polish bomber squadrons were eventually formed around the same time and with this expansion came a need for further Polish airmen to be trained. Newton was one of the stations chosen for this purpose.

With the departure of the Wellington squadrons, Gp Cpt J L Kepinski arrived to command No 16 (Polish) Service Flying Training School, which had arrived from Hucknall. This was not the first all-Polish unit to form. During the Battle of Britain, No 302 (Poznanski) Squadron had formed on 13th July 1940, was equipped with Hurricanes and quickly drawn into the battle. Having experienced the terrors of Nazi occupation, the Poles were particularly fearless and dedicated, almost to the point of fanaticism. They had one wish: to reap revenge for their homeland and kill Germans.

It was with this intent that the first Polish trainees arrived at Newton. They found an airfield that also accommodated No 722 Defence Command of the RAF, which comprised C Company of 10th Battalion of the Sherwood Foresters and the 112th Battery of the 28th Regiment, Royal Artillery, together with No 16 Works Flight of the RAF. Many had no knowledge of the English language and therefore had to attend classes in basic English. Encouraged by the CO, Gp Cpt E B Grenfell and the Polish CO, Sqn Ldr A W C S Skarzynski, what they learnt of the language was fine, many of them acquiring a good vocabulary. That is, until they were in the air, when the adrenalin began to flow and they got very excited. All that good English was lost and they reverted back to Polish to the dismay of the controllers in the operations room.

The unit was equipped with a selection of aircraft. Battles,

1. SCRAMBLE ~ START DO NATYCHMIASTOWEGO...
2. ANGL ~ ...
3. VECTOR ~ Zmienić kurs na...
4. BUSTER ~ lecieć pełną szybkością
5. LINER ~ zmniejszyć szyb. do ekonomicznej
6. GATE ~ lecieć max. szyb. 5 na stop. zm...
7. ORBIT ~ krążyć i obserwować
8. BOGEY ~ Nieznany sam. może być swoim
9. TALLY HO ~ Zaczynać drogę
10. BANDIT ~ Nieprzyjaciel, ustalono ilość i k.
11. PANCAKE ~ Powracaj i ląduj.

Polish English lessons depicting RAF language when in the air. (Crown)

Oxfords, DH60 Moths, Moth Minors, all were there for the purpose of training. As usual there was to be a number of incidents, one of which brought death to three Polish airmen. On 25th November 1941, several Battles were airborne with instructors and pupils. It was a routine training flight that ended in tragedy when Battle 2177 collided in mid-air with Battle 7407 at around 14.00 hours. As one Battle sliced the wings off the other, Fg Off S Dubas, an instructor, and LAC S Waskowiak, a pupil, fell to their deaths together with the pupil in the other Battle, LAC E Manka. Saddened by their deaths, the unit put on a ceremony the next day when a visit by the Polish Inspector General, Air Vice Marshal Vjejski, accompanied by Air Vice Marshal R P Willock and Gp Cpt The Lord Douglas Hamilton took place. In his speech, the Inspector General told the assembled station that he was devastated by the news of the deaths and thanked them for displaying such devotion to duty at a very difficult time.

Such was the intensity of the training that a satellite airfield was very soon required. Sutton Bridge was the chosen field but with the increase in flying hours, a further Relief Landing Ground was established at Tollerton. During 1942 further

Semi-sunk Operations Room at RAF Newton. Though closed for the last two years, the site is remarkably well kept. (Author)

pressure was put upon the training units, leading to more tragedies. On 4th May Corporal J Kuchta was killed, with LAC F Zawaoski sustaining severe injuries, when their Tiger Moth flew into high tension cables whilst practising low level flying techniques.

Since their arrival in the area, the Poles had integrated within the community fairly well. They had found their favourite pubs; in the case of Nottingham it was the 'Flying Horse'. Many had acquired old cars, some of which would not have passed today's MOT. They found the English girls delightful and with many of their own men away in the forces, there was no shortage of takers. The Midlands countryside afforded many opportunities for extra rations, with poaching becoming one of the main sources. Chickens, rabbits, fish, eggs, all became fair game. Whilst some farmers would tend to turn a blind eye to the Polish activities, the station Warrant Officer often did not!

April 1943 saw the more modern Miles Magisters and Avro Ansons arrive. The latter was the first twin-engined training aircraft that the Poles were to fly. Later in the month, Gp Cpt E B Grenfell AFC arrived to command Newton as the training intensified even more. The training really began on the Link Trainer, the 1940s equivalent of today's simulators. This wingless contraption allowed the feeling of real flying to be experienced without leaving the ground. It banked, it turned, it dived and it flew straight and level, each movement being monitored at the control panel a short distance away. Once hours had been spent inside the Link, the pupils went on to a proper aircraft alongside a flying instructor. As time went on, so the language problem improved to the satisfaction of the operations room.

The new year of 1944 saw a brief period when Newton became un-serviceable due to the heavy demands being made upon its grass. Consequently some flying in the early part of the year was carried out at the satellite at Sutton Bridge. This allowed the grass to re-grow and by the end of March the airfield was once again serviceable.

No 16 SFTS was joined by No 1524 Blind Approach Training Flight on 6th June. The Airspeed Oxfords soon became a familiar sight around the county with their display of yellow triangles on the fuselage and wings. The flight was particularly conspicious due to the fact that the unit carried a black letter on the fuselage triangles, eg Oxford DF347 'J'. Most other BAT flights sported white, sky or pale blue letters. With the arrival of the Oxfords, a new satellite was opened at Orston to accommodate the increase in flying.

Yet another aircraft was introduced to the Poles when a number of North American Harvards arrived. First delivered to the RAF in December 1938, the Harvard remained standard equipment at Flying Training Schools for over sixteen years. No 16 SFTS received the Harvard IIB, which was built by Noorduyn in Canada and corresponded to the USAAF's AT-6A. The aircraft proved a favourite with the Poles once they had got used to the rasping sound of the single Pratt and Whitney Wasp engine. The noise was the result of the tips of the propeller reaching almost supersonic speed. Though it endeared itself to the Poles, it goes without saying that it did not appeal to the local population.

As the run-down to victory continued, 2nd October 1944 saw British troops land in Crete while Aachen became the first German town to fall into the hands of the allies. In the light of the news, Christmas 1944 was celebrated at Newton with more gusto than in previous years. Although victory was in sight, the demand for aircrew was just as great. No 16 SFTS continued training the Polish aircrew on the same level. This was to continue after VE day, 8th May 1945, and it was not until October 1946 that a signal was received to close the school down. For five years it had provided a core of trained aircrew for the operational squadrons, but with the peace, demand had diminished very quickly. With its closure came the news that Newton was to become a station in No 12 Group, Fighter Command with the group headquarters transferring to Newton at the same time. The training aircraft left, to be replaced by aircraft of No 12 Group Communications Flight. Nineteen forty-seven saw the establishment of the Nottingham University Air Squadron, later to become the East Midlands University Air Squadron. The UAS and the Army Grading School were the last to fly fixed wing aircraft from Newton, moving out to Cranwell and Middle Wallop, respectively, in 2000. Transfer to Technical Training Command in August 1958 brought the guided weapons training to Newton, with the electrical and instrument training centre arriving in 1964.

Peacetime brought many and rapid changes to the base, a good number of them connected with the Air Training Corps. No 644 Gliding School and the Air Cadet Central Gliding School arrived

One of the 'C' type hangars at RAF Newton. (Author)

to carry out glider training and air experience flights, all of these units being linked with the parent unit at nearby Syerston. It became the headquarters of the Air Training Corps, a position it held until the 1990s.

Of the Polish airmen who trained at Newton during the war, 42 were to be awarded British decorations for courage in action and meritorious service. The connection between the Free Polish Forces and RAF Newton was so strong that a white Polish eagle was incorporated in the peacetime station crest. The station has now closed as a military base. It survives (in 2003) as the largest grass airfield in the East Midlands.

13

OSSINGTON

National Grid Reference SK745648, 8 miles NW of Newark

In the opening chapters we have read about the advantages of a decoy airfield. Many similar wartime airfields did not have this facility, yet it was decided by the Air Ministry that Ossington should. This was duly set up at Upton though this position placed it closer to Gamston. Thus, it may well have served a dual purpose, with the overriding factor being that Ossington should become a major bomber airfield.

Sited 8 miles NW of Newark, construction began in 1941 with a preliminary finish date of early 1942. Laid out as a standard bomber airfield, it had three hard runways, the longest being 4,980 feet and the shortest 2,770 feet. Accommodation and technical buildings were adequate and when completed it became an airfield within No 5 Group, Bomber Command. Like so many of the Nottinghamshire airfields, however, it did not become a front-line bomber station, but instead, in January 1942, became a base within Flying Training Command. No 14 (Pilot) AFU equipped with Airspeed Oxfords moved in and began pilot training. For the next 15 months, the unit became a familiar sight around Nottingham, but a change of command for Ossington in May 1942 saw them move to Banff in Scotland.

Reverting back to Bomber Command and No 93 Group, the airfield was given Gamston as a satellite airfield. On 1st June 1943 No 82 OTU formed with the usual complement of Wellington Mk.III and X aircraft, together with five Miles Martinets that were used for drogue towing. They were tasked with training air gunners and also used for air affiliation

126

exercises with fighters. June and July were accident free months but, sadly, this was to change on 9th August when a crew were lost through no fault of their own. Wellington X MS471 was on a cross-country exercise having taken off from Ossington during the afternoon. When it was on the return leg and flying at low level, the starboard engine failed. Despite the valiant efforts of Plt Off W Adams to remain airborne, the Wellington crashed on the main road leading to Newark. Sadly, the entire crew, Plt Off W Adams, Plt Off F Graham-Bell, Plt Off H Ibbott RCAF, Sgt R W Ballauff and Sgt P Baldwin, perished in the ensuing fire. Death came once again on 21st August when another Wellington X, HE332, was also flying a cross-country exercise with an all-NCO crew. Arriving back at Ossington, the aircraft collided with trees as it turned onto its final approach, resulting in the deaths of Flt Sgt F G Ingham and Sgt R W Hughes and injuries to Flt Sgt H O Shaw RAAF and Flt Sgt E A McCasker RCAF.

It appears that the Harrogate Cemetery was the final resting place for many of the OTU crews operating from both Ossington and Gamston. A further five were interned there when Wellington III BK387 encountered mist and low cloud and crashed into high ground at Tewitt Hall Wood. Sadly, WO2 E I Glass, Fg Off J J McHenry, WO2 J E Dalling, WO2 J Henfrey, Sgt N W Crawford and Sgt E Savage, all of the RCAF, lost their lives. As 1944 wore on, they would be joined by many others as the pressures of intense training took their toll.

An incident of a different kind with rather more satisfying results occurred on 22nd May 1944 when Fg Off Lee of the RCAF was flying Wellington III BJ819 on a cine camera gun detail. The Wellington was flying in conjunction with a Spitfire I, P7820 from No 53 OTU. An unavoidable collision occurred between the two aircraft with both crash-landing in a field at Leverton. At the subsequent Court of Inquiry, praise was given to the pilot, Fg Off Lee when it was discovered that his actions in landing safely had saved his entire crew. For this it was recommended that a 'green' endorsement should be written up in his log book.

In June the OTU was joined by No 1685 Training Flight equipped with the Curtiss Tomahawk. They stayed only for a brief time before Ossington once again became an OTU base. The rate of accidents at this time had slowed as a gradual run-down of some of the OTUs was taking place. No 82 were to continue until January 1945, when they were disbanded. Ossington was

```
                                    Appendix 1 to Form 540
                                    R.A.F. Station, Ossington.
                                    January, 1945.


          REPORT BY THE CHIEF GROUND INSTRUCTOR

                     on the work of

          No. 6 LANCASTER FINISHING SCHOOL
                  ─────────────────


     The formation of No. 6 Lancaster Finishing School at R.A.F.
Station, Ossington was commenced with the planning of the Training
Wing, which started on 14th December, 1944.

     Progress was somewhat hampered by the fact that No. 82 O.T.U.
of Bomber Command was still functioning and instructional accom-
modation could only be taken over as the various sections completed
their final commitment.

     In addition to this much delay was experienced because instruc-
tors and equipment did not arrive when anticipated.  However,
the work went ahead and the ground school, although not completely
equipped, was ready to start the first course on the target date:
15th January, 1945.

     Twenty-three Pilots, 12 Navigators and 12 Radio Operators
commenced training.  It is intended at the end of the first
three weeks training to select 12 Pilots, 6 Navigators and 6
Radio Operators to continue training as No. 1 Course.  The residue
will form into No. 2 Course and re-start the course.

     Five students of the initial intake were not acceptable to
British Overseas Airways Corporation on medical grounds and
disposal action is being taken.

     The anticipated output date for No. 1 Course is 19th March,
1945 but it is feared that an extension for the course will have
to be requested in order to allow the students to reach the
licence standard required by British Overseas Airways Corporation.

     The complete training time-table has not yet been produced
but is being compiled from week to week as training proceeds.
A full nine-week programme will be submitted with next month's
Training Summary.
```

A report on the work of No 6 Lancaster Finishing School at RAF Ossington. (PRO-Air 28/606)

transferred to Transport Command awaiting the arrival of No 6 LFS. Operated by the command and BOAC, its role was to train Lancaster pilots to operate Lancastrians (Lancasters converted for civil use) on the UK to New Zealand route. A notice similar to the modern NOTAM (Notice to all airmen) was placed for all to read. It stated 'January 15th 1945. No 6 Lancaster Finishing School is a training school operated jointly by Transport Command and British Overseas Airways Corporation. The immediate purpose of the school is to train 72 aircrew who will operate Lancastrian aircraft on the London to New Zealand route. The course is of 9 weeks duration, 7 weeks ground and 2 flying'. On 16th March, No 1 course had completed training and eight pilots, three navigators and five radio operators reached the standard required for secondment to BOAC. On 1st November 1945, it was renamed No 1384 Heavy Transport Conversion Unit and incorporated Avro York aircraft in addition to the Lancastrian. Still a military airfield, Ossington was now commanded by Gp Cpt P W Johnson, who oversaw training until May 1946 when, with the arrival of better civilian aircraft and more company training, the unit closed down and Ossington was left to the elements. The hard runways were broken up for hardcore needed for the rapidly growing housing developments, and the base entered the history books. As with all the OTUs, it had played its part in defeating the enemy

14

PAPPLEWICK MOOR

National Grid Reference SK550510, 6 miles N of Nottingham,
immediately E of Linby

This base was activated in the First World War as a relief landing ground for No 15 Training Depot Station (later 15 Training School from March 1919), which had been formed at Hucknall on 1 April 1918. The site was just a grass strip with no permanent buildings and was used for circuit, landing and take-off practice by pilots under training. With the end of the First World War the RAF was rapidly run down and Papplewick Moor was returned to its farmer owner in 1919. Aircraft likely to have flown from here include DH6, DH9 and Avro 504K types.

With the Second World War demanding more and more air-strips, the Air Ministry looked for suitable sites for relief landing grounds again and checked all the abandoned ones, pressing many back into service. Although very small this strip was requisitioned and immediately brought back into military service as an emergency landing ground to No 1 (Polish) Flying Training School, in No 21 Group, Flying Training Command, based at Hucknall with Tiger Moths and twin-engined Oxford trainers. However, Papplewick Moor suffered from trees along one boundary and electricity cables along another, making it far from suitable for flying. Nevertheless it was used extensively, although often the aircraft would only make an approach and not actually land because of the obstructions around the site. In January 1941 the School absorbed the Polish Testing & Grading Flight from

A pristine Miles Magister seen at a post-war air display. Many pupil pilots had their training on this type. (M. J. Giddings)

Kirkbride and Carlisle and their Battles and Magisters moved to Hucknall and started to be seen here. In July 1941 No 25 (Polish) Elementary Flying Training School moved to Hucknall and also utilised this strip as a relief landing ground for its Tiger Moths. Nearby Firbeck and Blidworth were also used for the same purpose. Virtually no buildings were erected at Papplewick Moor but it kept this role until November 1945, when No 25 EFTS disbanded. In the meantime No 1 (Polish) FTS had been renamed No 16 FTS on 9 June 1941 but still undertook basic flying training on Tiger Moths at Hucknall. Many local relief landing grounds were used by this unit, which disbanded in December 1946, having by then given up this strip. Papplewick Moor remained in use by No 25 EFTS until November 1945, when that unit relocated, changed its name and gave up this satellite. Two buildings remain but otherwise no trace of this airfield can be seen.

15
SYERSTON

National Grid Reference SK730480, 6 miles SW of Newark

The first Polish decoration to be awarded to a Polish airman in Great Britain did not go to one of the Polish fighter aces but to an armourer of No 301 (Pomorski) Bomber Squadron. The citation read: 'On 18th September 1940, Sergeant S Nowak was unloading the bomb rack of a plane that had returned from an operation. Whilst doing so, the fuse on a flare bomb caught on something and the safety catch blew out. Sgt Nowak, knowing that there were three fitters inside the aircraft and despite a wounded shoulder, took the bomb in both arms and ran 15 yards to open ground where it exploded nearly killing him. With this action he saved three other lives.' The Polish bomber squadrons did not receive the glory or publicity that the fighters did but two were to serve with distinction for seven months at the Nottinghamshire airfield of Syerston.

The airfield lay 6 miles SW of Newark-on-Trent and was one of the last permanent stations to be built before the war. Opening on 1st December 1940, it was a bomber station in No 1 Group of Bomber Command and was commanded by Gp Cpt Wilfrid Sanderson AFC. That it was intended to be a major base is denoted by the fact that it had a satellite airfield at Balderton and a night decoy airfield at Kneeton, two miles SW of Syerston. No time was wasted in using the airfield as, one day later, on 2nd December, two Polish bomber squadrons, Nos 304 (Silesian) and 305 (Wielpolska), arrived from Bramcote. No 304 was the third Polish bomber squadron to form in Britain as part of No 6 (Training) Group, Bomber Command with many of the

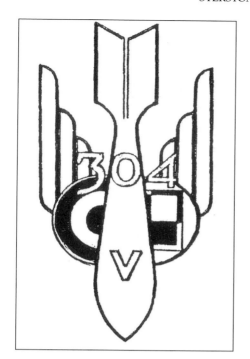

No 304 Squadron's badge.
(Chris Samson)

personnel having previously served in the 2nd and 6th Air Regiments in Poland. The design of the squadron badge was chosen by competition among members of the squadron and showed a falling bomb with wings marked 'V' (for Victory) and the number 304. Below, emblems of the RAF and Polish Air Force each side of the bomb, half of a red, white and blue RAF roundel, level with half of a white and red Polish chequerboard. The first Polish CO was Wg Cdr Jan Bialy with acting Wg Cdr William Monteith Graham as the British advisor.

No 305 followed a similar pattern, with many personnel of the 3rd (Poznan) and 5th (Lida) Air Regiments within its ranks. Their squadron badge showed a Hussar's wing facing left containing the Field Marshal's Baton and his initials J. P. The No 305 was at the base of the badge in the wing feathers; a quarter of the Polish Air Force chequerboard was shown above a quarter of an RAF roundel. Their first Polish CO was Wg Cdr (Navig) Jan Jankowski with Wg Cdr James K M Drysdale DSO as the RAF squadron adviser.

No 304 Squadron had recently converted from Battles to the

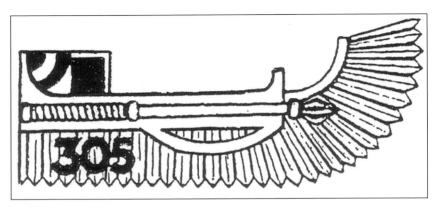

No 305 Squadron's badge. (Chris Samson)

Wellington Ic, whilst 305 were still equipped with the Battle. Both squadrons' personnel were Poles who had escaped from France and North Africa and had arrived at Bramcote to form the two squadrons. They were a little unhappy that after becoming operational on the Battle they would have to re-train on the Wellington. Consequently the inevitable accidents began, with one of the first being on 14th December 1940, when a Wellington of 304 Squadron took off to carry out a cross-country training flight. Due to very low cloud, the pilot decided to come down below the cloud base and unfortunately flew into the side of a hill at West Edmondsley. The pilot, Fg Off Waroczewski, sustained a fractured wrist and facial injuries. Fg Off Kostuck damaged his arm and face, Fg Off Stanczuk had leg and face injuries whilst Sgt Boczkowski received chest and face injuries. The entire crew were lucky not to have been killed.

The arrival of Wg Cdr Dudzinski on 19th December to take command of the Polish element in the two squadrons indicated that the training was on-going. At the end of 1940 the station diarist was able to record: 'Considerable progress in the organisation of the station was made during the month and training in the squadrons proceeded satisfactorily although handicapped by lack of equipment and personnel.'

On 27th January 1941, the King and Queen visited the station. Representing a grateful British nation, they were accompanied by Air Marshal Sir Richard Pierse, CB, DSO, AFC, who was then Commander-in-Chief of Bomber Command. Both spoke in glowing terms of the loyalty and determination of the Polish airmen and the visit was received with great acclaim by the squadrons who put on a display of their homeland for the visitors to see. One unusual member of 305 on parade that day was the squadron mascot, a terrier-type dog by the name of Ciapek, pronounced in English 'Chapek'. On parade he marched quietly to heel behind the CO. Accorded the rank of Corporal, he flew with the Wellington crews on operations to Berlin, Bremen, Munich and many more German cities. The airmen had contrived a special parachute fixed to a sheepskin harness and an oxygen respirator for use at high altitudes. On his last 'mission', he was the sole survivor when the Wellington he was flying in crashed. He was found weeks later on the shore at Cromer, Norfolk, identified by his special collar but, unfortunately, unable to report the fate of his crew.

For the Polish airmen the royal visit was indeed an honour as both their Majesties spoke to many of them. Four days later a message was received from the C-in-C, Bomber Command relaying a letter he had received from the King. 'We have just returned deeply impressed and encouraged by our visit to squadrons in your command.'

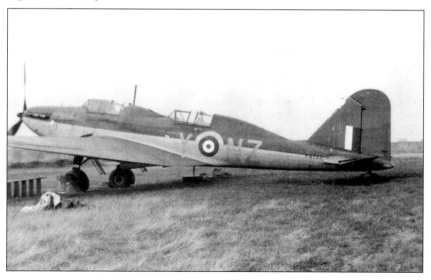

A training Fairey Battle of No 304 (Polish) Squadron, RAF Syerston. (RAF Museum PO17883)

135

The first visit by the enemy took place on 14th March, when, at 23.57 hours, nine short delay bombs were dropped by enemy aircraft flying at a height of 500 to 1,000 feet. They all exploded on the landing ground creating two craters 25ft in diameter and 15 feet deep. Though they caused severe damage no loss of life was reported. Such was the indignation of the station defence personnel that the enemy should attack their airfield that two machine gun posts fired consistently at the aircraft. They were joined by fire from two Armadillo armoured cars which had raced round the perimeter, but no hits were registered on the enemy.

The conversion of the Polish squadrons took until April 1941, when they were deemed ready to go operational. Command of 304 had passed to Wg Cdr Piotr Dudzinski whilst command of 305 went to Wg Cdr (Pilot) Bohdan Kleczynski. Then, night after night as dusk fell, they would take off to deliver their bomb loads. The Wellingtons, laden with bombs and fuel, would struggle to get airborne. As they gained height to cross the Channel, the gunners would test their guns. Reaching 10,000 feet, oxygen masks would be worn as the crews prepared for the worst. As they crossed the coast of France or Belgium searchlights would begin to probe the night air. Once over the target it was flak, searchlights and nightfighters to worry about; then with the bombs dropped it was a turn for home with still more worries. Crossing back over Europe and enemy-held territory, the enemy nightfighters would be waiting for any lame ducks that were having problems. Those crews that did have problems ie, flak or gun hits, would be frantically worrying about whether they would make England or not. These feelings would be repeated night after night throughout the war, for, as the records show, the first operational flight by Polish bombers was from Swinderby on 14th September 1940 and the last was from Lincolnshire on 26th November 1946.

With very little airfield control at this period, accidents were bound to happen. One such tragedy occurred on 12th June 1941. Due to very bad visibility, a collision between Wellington R1017 and an Airspeed Oxford T1334 had resulted in the tragic loss of all occupants of both aircraft. The all-Polish crews were Flt Lt Stefanicki, Fg Off Kowalcze, Fg Off Wojtowicz, Fg Off Zirkwitz and Sgts Mruk and Kraweski. With a guard of honour from Syerston, they were buried with full military honours in the

Polish cemetery at Newark. Sadly, the student pilot of the Oxford, LAC William Robson Newton, was also killed in the accident.

The arrival of the Polish airmen at Syerston aroused mixed feelings in the local community. With time to kill between operations, the Poles would be seen in the local towns and villages *'en masse'*. One favourite haunt was the Flying Horse in Nottingham, a pub they almost made into Little Poland. It was here that the local girls would flock in the hope of finding a few hours' respite from the traumas of the war and, for many, working in the war industries. The Polish 'black market' became apparent and flourished, for it was not difficult for them to acquire all manner of rationed food and materials. The local farmers were only too anxious to trade with them for a drum of gasoline, smuggled out of Syerston.

By now, Bomber Command was entering a new phase of attack, that of saturation bombing. Fresh crews were appearing direct from the OTUs to replace losses. The number of these

The unveiling of the Polish memorial at Newark cemetery in Nottinghamshire. (IWM CH3000)

continued to rise as the chances of surviving a tour dropped to one in four. The devotion and loyalty of the Polish airmen did not go unnoticed when on 11th June 1941, Air Marshal Sir Richard E C Peirse and Acting Air Vice-Marshal R D Oxland visited Syerston and inspected Nos. 304 and 305. On 13th June 1941, the day after the previously mentioned loss of the six aircrew and student pilot, the two squadrons received a visit from the Duke of Kent and telegrams and citations from Bomber Command and the Air Ministry. The next day all four Polish squadrons paraded at the cemetery at Newark where so many of their colleagues were buried. The ceremony was held in the presence of President Wladyslaw Raczkiewicz and Prime Minister General Sikorski, both laying wreaths at the monument. Two days later, General Sikorski handed over the new Standard of the Polish Air Force to No 300 Squadron at Swinderby. It carried the words 'Love Demands Sacrifice'. In the coming months it would certainly demand that.

As the bombing of mainland Europe continued, so the losses increased. To mention just two incidents, the night of 18th/19th June saw an attack on Bremen. On the homeward journey, Wellington R1696 SM, twice suffered fighter attack and was finally shot down over Aschendorf. Of the crew, Fg Off Kazimierz Zerebecki died outright with Sgt Henryk Rogowski dying later that day in hospital. Two further crew, Fg Off Zerebecki and Sgt Rogowski, were both killed and were buried in the Netherlands, whilst Flt Lt Kazimierz Jaklewicz and Sgts Mieczyslaw Debkowski, Stanislaw Lewek and Edward Olonyn were taken prisoners. In 1944, in a POW journal, Flt Lt Jaklewicz wrote about the dying moments of his aircraft: 'A bright cloudless June night: a hail of bullets, fire in engines and fuselage: explosion of oxygen bottles, death of two crew members and finally a jump into the black, dismal depth of night below me and the outline of the Dutch coast: then the usual route to behind barbed wire.' On 24th June 1941, ten aircraft attacked Cologne and Boulogne. Although the weather was good, one of the aircraft detailed to attack the latter failed to return. Due to the fact that one of the other crews had seen the aircraft go down in the Channel, the air-sea rescue launch was despatched but, sadly, found only the body of Sqd Ldr Kielich in the water. The Polish squadrons pressed home their attacks relentlessly but 1941 was to see 244 Polish men perish, representing two thirds of their strength. Such was their hatred of the enemy that many took on

No 408 (Goose) Sqdn with one of their Hampdens at Syerston in 1942.
(408 Sqdn via V. Baker)

extra tours when they should have been resting. However, word had been received that the squadrons were to leave Syerston in the foreseeable future. Accordingly, on 19th July 1941, No 304 moved to Lindholme, followed by No 305 a day later. It was a sorrowful day for the Poles, who had come to regard Syerston as home. Now they were to carry on the fight with better and newer marks of Wellingtons, and No 305 Squadron were destined to move to France after D-Day.

Hours after No 304 had left, No 408 (Goose) Squadron of the Royal Canadian Air Force flew its ageing Handley Page Hampdens into Syerston for a long stay. This aircraft, along with the Wellington, bore the brunt of Bomber Command's early raids over Germany. It was a medium bomber carrying a crew of four and powered by two 1,000hp Bristol Pegasus engines. Handley Page were responsible for building 500 Hampdens, but others (770) were sub-contracted to The English Electric Company Ltd, whilst a number were built in Canada by The Canadian Association Aircraft Ltd.

Suddenly the population of Syerston and the surrounding area had to get used to a Canadian drawl instead of the guttural Polish of late. The squadron spent the rest of July on settling into

The crew and ground crew of a Stirling are dwarfed by the wing size. (Crown)

A typical scene at every bomber airfield, selecting bombs for the night's operation. (Crown)

a flying training programme with the first mission being carried out over the night of 11th/12th August 1941. This was a low key attack on the docks at Rotterdam, from which all aircraft returned safely. One of the problems with the Hampden was that it carried such a small bomb load. Although armed with one fixed and one movable 0.303 gun forward and twin 0.303 guns in dorsal and ventral positions, the maximum bomb load was 4,000lbs. Compared with the Short Stirlings, which carried a load

141

of 14,000lbs and was a four-engined and large bomber in service very shortly after the Hampden, it is easy to see just why the Hampden was soon relegated to lesser operations. No 408, however, put their aircraft to good use whilst at Syerston and it is perhaps appropriate here to take the reader through a typical run-up procedure to an operation.

Out on the airfield the groundcrews are preparing the Hampdens for the night's bombing operation. The engine fitters are checking the engines and oil consumption against the pilot's log. Bomb racks are examined prior to bombing up whilst an electrical fitter checks all the electrical systems. Controls are tested and tyres are pumped up. When all this is done it is time to refuel and re-arm the aircraft to its maximum.

Meanwhile the aircrew are attending a briefing to see what the target is for tonight. They sit facing a raised platform behind which is a blackboard and a map of Europe, usually covered over. Will it be Rotterdam, Antwerp or a target in Germany? All is revealed as the Squadron Commander and Intelligence officer lift the covering. Once revealed, notes are taken before particulars are given of possible enemy opposition, eg flak, searchlights, enemy aircraft and balloons. The crew are then addressed in turn by the signals officer and the weather man. Some briefings last 15 minutes, others 30 minutes depending on the information required.

Once the briefing is over, the crews get together to work out a flight plan. Captains will check their aircraft externally with the groundcrews and see that it is serviceable and ready to go before the aircrews go for a meal and wait for nightfall. As dusk approaches, they change into their flying clothes before joining the transport to take them to their aircraft. With the Captain taking a last minute check around the aircraft to make sure all is well, the rest of the crew climb aboard and test their systems. Although each aircraft is test flown during the afternoon, sometimes, over a space of time, systems can go wrong. Once all this is completed and clearance is given to taxi, a very worrying and cold few hours begin, continuing until the aircraft is back on its home station again.

Relentlessly the squadron continued its nightly bombing attacks. As autumn 1941 approached, it was rumoured that Syerston was to undergo major re-construction as the large four-engined bombers came into service. On 9th December, No 408

Squadron took their Hampdens to Balderton as Syerston closed for work to start on laying two hard runways, together with hardstandings and further accommodation. Two runways 1,430 yards long were built together with a main runway of 1,900 yards in length. This work took until May 1942, when the airfield re-opened as a heavy bomber station.

For the permanent staff left at Syerston, the diarist recorded the Christmas period in minute detail: 'The usual festivities took place today and Christmas fare was provided for all left on the station. The Sergeants were entertained in the Officers mess in the morning and, as is customary, the Officers and Sergeants waited upon the airmen in their mess. Flt Lt Reid, the press officer, accompanied by CBC made a recording of the Christmas dinner festivities for transmission to Canada.'

The reporter also recorded one operation carried out by 408 Squadron, which took place on 10th January 1942 whilst flying from Balderton. Ten Hampdens of the squadron had been detailed to carry out an attack on the railway station at Wilhelmshaven. Taking off between 16.38 hours and 16.55 hours, the crews found cloud over the target, together with a lot of flak. The first aircraft did not identify the target correctly and instead dropped his bombs on the town. The second bombed a flak concentration, while a third dropped his bombs on the docks. With a fourth aircraft detailed to drop leaflets, the rest of the squadron did not find the target either and jettisoned their bombs over the North Sea. It was a rough ride back, with heavy gunfire and a lot of flak. Several aircraft were holed by the latter, Plt Off Brown bringing his aircraft back on one engine. Out of the ten Hampdens, one, flown by Flt Lt T F Priest, failed to return.

In April 1942, No 61 Squadron began converting to the Avro Lancaster I from the much maligned twin-engined Avro Manchester. Conversion took place at Woolfox Lodge until on 5th May 1942 they brought their Lancasters to Syerston. After many problems with the Manchester, the crews at last felt that they had an aircraft they could rely on. Apart from a detachment that was sent to St Eval in Cornwall, the squadron began an extensive training programme prior to carrying out the first operations. Once they began their bombing sorties, night after night would see them flying to destroy the Nazi industrial might. Targets like Hamburg and Bremen, Dusseldorf and Hanover all became familiar to the crews. Attacks on these and other industrial targets became the work for No 61 Squadron and many others. The squadron motto, *'Per Purum Tonantes'* – Thundering through the Clear Sky – became very apt. Meanwhile, a new C-in-C had arrived at Bomber Command. Air Marshal A T Harris had ideas of his own regarding hitting back at the German heartland. He believed that saturation bombing would help to bring a quicker end to the war. In this respect, by 18th May, he had formalised plans for the first ever 1,000 bomber raid over Germany. Its intention was to annihilate one of the enemy's main industrial centres by fire. The target was Cologne.

With the bomber force including training groups, army co-operation, flying training and Coastal Command, it was to be an all-out effort. No 61 Squadron were to be included and on the eve of 30th/31st May, the Lancasters were prepared and made ready for this, the first great raid of the war. As the armada took off from their different airfields, No 61 left Syerston to join them. The attack took place in three waves. Led by the Wellingtons of No 3 Group, the Stirlings came next followed by the Manchesters and Lancasters of No 5 Group. From miles away, the third wave could see the fires of Cologne making the sky appear red. As they flew over the city to drop their bombs, the crews of 61 could not believe their eyes. They had never seen fires like it before. With the deed done it was a turn away and head for home. The next day *The Times* headline ran: 'Over 1,000 bombers raid Cologne. Biggest attack of the war. 2,000 tons of bombs in 40 minutes.' Forty-one crews were lost, 24 from the squadrons and 17 from training units. With so many aircraft in the sky at one time, these numbers were seen by the Command as a justifiable risk. One aircraft from 61 Squadron, sadly, did not return from Cologne due to a mid-air collision (see the Balderton chapter). Weary crews landed back at Syerston, gave their reports to the intelligence officer, went over to the mess for a meal and then to bed. It had been quite a night.

On 30th September, Syerston became a two squadron bomber station with the arrival of No 106 Squadron from Coningsby. The advance party had arrived on 28th September to be followed by the main party and aircraft two days later. Also 106 had contributed to the Cologne raid but without their Commanding Officer, Wg Cdr Guy Penrose Gibson. He had, unfortunately, been hospitalised due to a possible ear infection. The usual 'beat up' of Coningsby had taken place as they left and flew cross country to Syerston. Greeted by the Station Commander, Gp Cpt Augustus Walker, Gibson and 106 settled into their new station and began a series of low level flying exercises. On 17th October the reason for the low level work became apparent when an attack on the Schneider Armament and Locomotive Works at Le Creusot took place. The raid was exclusively 5 Group's with 94 Lancasters forming up soon after midday. No 106 squadron supplied ten aircraft, which were led by Gibson. The target was reached shortly after 18.00 hours as the aircraft formed up to bomb in turn. The raid lasted 9 minutes, with the force dropping over 200 tons of high explosive bombs together with incendiaries. Huge fires were seen to erupt and the entire area was soon blanketed in thick black smoke. All the aircraft returned to their bases safely, the only damage being to Gibson's, which was slightly holed by flak, and Flt Lt Hopgood's whose aircraft was damaged by his own bombs exploding. He must have been flying very low!

Four nights later the target was Genoa in Italy. This entailed a round trip of 9½ hours. Again it was a success, with the target being well lit by the Pathfinder Squadron that preceded the main bomber force. This raid was a prelude to the start of the Western Desert offensive, which started the very next day. For 106, it was Italy again, this time during daylight. The crews scattered leaflets in addition to bombs, warning the Italians that the end of Mussolini's reign was near. The next day saw Gibson and 106 Squadron yet again flying out to bomb – this time Milan. With good sunny conditions, the crews had a lovely view of the Alps as they crossed them, the weather becoming very warm as they flew south. Once over, they dropped down to bombing level and released their load. Below, people could be seen running to the shelters in panic, but the objective to bomb was purely military and not civilian. All the aircraft returned safely to Syerston. Italy seemed to be the prime target for both the squadrons around this time and by November it became obvious just why. On the eighth of the month, North Africa was invaded. The allies had begun the fight back.

For Syerston's other squadron, No 61, the targets had also been in Italy. With both squadrons flying intensive operations, accidents were bound to occur, as the evening of 8th December showed. The target was Turin and Syerston provided twelve aircraft from 61 Squadron and eleven from 106. On this occasion,

No 106 Squadron at Syerston in September 1942. Guy Gibson is centre front on the right of the dog mascot. (RAF Museum P016121)

Gibson was not flying and watched with horror the scene unfolding before his eyes. On the far side of the airfield stood a Lancaster of 61 Squadron which was a reserve aircraft for use should any of the main force become unserviceable. Its bomb bay held 41 incendiaries and a 4,000lb 'Cookie'; and its bomb doors were open. As the other aircraft taxied close by the vibration they created caused the incendiaries to fall out of the bay, with some igniting on contact with the ground. The station CO, Gus Walker, and Gibson saw them ignite and, fearing a holocaust, the CO ran to his car and sped off in the direction of the Lancaster to warn the crew still sitting on board. Reaching the aircraft, he got out of his car and was running towards the Lancaster to pull the incendiary rack clear of it when the 4,000lb bomb exploded. The explosion shot upwards to what appeared to be about 2,000 feet, with fire and red hot pieces of bomb casing shooting everywhere, Gp Cpt Walker lost his right arm below the elbow. Somehow he managed to walk to the ambulance that had followed him before passing out and being taken to the station sick bay. Ten other men were also badly injured, but good and quick work by the doctor ensured that they were all made comfortable before being taken to the Annexe Theatre at Rauceby. Such was the spirit, however, of the CO that when Gibson visited him in hospital, he asked if he would search for his arm. Apparently it had a brand new glove on it! Two months later, Gp Cpt Walker returned to resume the role of station commander, minus his arm.

It fell to Guy Gibson and his crew to drop the first 8,000lb bomb of the war. This took place on 28th November, the aircraft taking off at 19.00 hours and returning at 03.00 hours. Bombing from 800 feet, the crew were devastated to see the damage caused by one bomb; so much so that Gibson flew back and forth over the target area taking photos. When these were processed and shown to various Chiefs of Staff, they found it hard to comprehend that just one bomb could do so much damage – albeit an 8,000lb one.

As November 1942 drew to a close, it was time to take stock of operations so far. The month had proved very successful for No 106 for they had lost not one aircraft, despite a heavy flying schedule. Now, with the winter weather setting in, the pressure of constant operations would diminish slightly. Sad to say, during the month of December the squadron lost two aircraft. Bad weather over the Christmas period ensured that the crews were able to take some rest. Guy Gibson had been given a black Labrador pup, one of a litter that the bitch of a close friend from Gibson's West Malling days had produced. Named 'Nigger', it was later to go down in history as the inspiration for the code-word for the successful breach of the Mohne dam. For now, it was to become something resembling a squadron mascot and was to liven up the evenings in the mess.

One of the first operations of the new year took place on 16th January 1943, when 106 were detailed to bomb Berlin. Gibson's Lancaster was to carry a VIP in the form of Major Richard Dimbleby, the BBC war correspondent. It had been arranged for him to fly on this operation due to the fact that the target was the capital of Germany and the propaganda value would be immense. With the RAF now hitting at the heart of Germany, it was felt that a recorded mission to be broadcast later over the wireless would be good for civilian morale. This raid was a big one. A total of 201 aircraft would bomb the city with No 106 squadron putting forward thirteen. With tests and bombing and arming completed, the thirteen aircraft took off at 16.30 hours. As they climbed up and joined the main force, Richard Dimbleby was seen to pass out. A kink in his oxygen tube had been the culprit, but, with help from the flight engineer, he was restored to consciousness. As they crossed the enemy coast, the flak began to appear followed by the searchlights. Dimbleby appeared most enthusiastic about the entire scenario until one piece of flak exploded close to the Lancaster, causing it to be tossed about. Once over the target, Gibson was not satisfied that the aiming point could be seen and elected to go around three times. This motion caused Dimbleby to be violently sick. On the third run, the 8,000lb 'Cookie' was released and the aircraft turned for home. Several days later the recording was transmitted. As the members of 106 listened to the emotion and trauma of the operation that Dimbleby so elegantly portrayed in his recording, a glow of satisfaction emanated when he paid tribute to Bomber Command, Guy Gibson and the squadron in particular. It was a well deserved tribute to a fine unit.

Gibson had now completed 67 bombing raids and had been with 106 Squadron for eleven months. It is reported that he was showing signs of fatigue but refused to take a break. The success of the Dimbleby report had brought Syerston to the notice of the media and the base was to become well-known through various articles in newspapers. One in particular was printed in the *Sunday Express*, which ran the headline: '3 tons of bombs on Essen every 4 seconds for 35 minutes'. It was startling stuff, yet it told the British public just how Bomber Command was hitting back at the enemy.

The last flight that Guy Gibson made with 106 Squadron was to Stuttgart on 11th March 1943. The flight was not a good one to finish on, for on the outward journey his Lancaster lost an engine. Debating whether to press on or return to Syerston, he judged that they could manage on three engines and, anyway, he did not want to abort his last mission with the squadron. Arriving over the target and flying lower than the rest of the force, they bombed on the markers and turned for home. Now that the bomb had gone, the Lancaster had a new lease of life and the three engines allowed the aircraft to land safely at Syerston. His departure warranted a huge party, which did not end until the early hours of the morning. Intending to go on leave (or was he forced?), Guy was summoned to No 5 Group headquarters

Wing Commander Guy Gibson VC, DSO and Bar, DFC and Bar.

and asked if he would consider forming his own squadron for a top secret mission. This, of course, was to be No 617 Squadron and the German dams. Consequently, Guy did not go on leave. Under his leadership, No 106 had risen to be a top squadron in the group. For his work with them, Guy Penrose Gibson was awarded a bar to his DSO and a citation which read: 'This officer has an outstanding operational record, having completed 172 sorties. He has always displayed the greatest keenness and within the past two months has taken part in six attacks against well defended targets, including Berlin. By his skilled leadership and contempt for danger he has set an example which has inspired the squadron he commands.'

No 61 Squadron were also to hit the headlines whilst at Syerston when the award of the Victoria Cross to a member of the squadron lifted the spirits. The recipient of the award was Acting Flt Lt W Reid, who, whilst piloting Lancaster O Oboe on a raid to Dusseldorf, came under heavy attack from an enemy nightfighter. It was shortly after crossing the Dutch coast that an attack by an Me110 shattered his windscreen and caused Flt Lt Reid to suffer wounds in the head, shoulder and hands. Considerable damage was also done to the Lancaster, with the elevator trimming tabs shot away making it difficult to control. The rear gun turret was badly damaged and out of action and the intercom and compasses were not functioning. Speaking to a reporter whilst convalescing, Flt Lt Reid gave an account of how he felt. 'I just saw a blinding flash, the windscreen went and the aircraft lost about 2,000 feet before I could gain a little control. I could see very little and I felt as though my head had been blown off. Other members of the crew shouted to see if I was alright, but it was no good telling them that I felt half dead so I replied I was alright. I managed to resume my course again but I felt as though someone had hit me with a hammer. Blood was pouring down my face and I could feel the taste of it in my mouth. It soon froze though because of the intense cold'.

Shortly afterwards, the aircraft was attacked again and hit from stem to stem. In this attack the navigator was killed and the wireless operator fatally injured. The oxygen system was out of action and Reid was further wounded. The flight engineer, though himself hit in the arm by a bullet, supplied the pilot with oxygen from a portable supply. Flt Lt Reid continued: 'I looked for the Pole Star and flew on that for a bit. I knew from the flight

Flight Lieutenant William Reid VC. He gained his VC for heroism whilst a member of No 61 Squadron at Syerston. (IWM CHP794)

plan just roughly where we were. Then I could see Cologne on the starboard and turned for the attack on Dusseldorf'.

After the bombs had gone he steered a little north to avoid the many German defences and headed for home as best he could by the stars. He was by then growing weak from loss of blood and the emergency oxygen supply had run out. 'The elevators had been shot away and we had to hold back the stick the whole of the time, he continued. 'That was a tough job. We went through heavy flak near the Dutch coast and then I saw the searchlights over England. We were losing height all the time, but I knew that we were near the English coast and did not worry unduly. As we crossed over, I saw the lights of an airfield and proceeded to prepare to land. Just as we touched down the undercarriage collapsed and we went along on our tummy for about 50 yards. Fortunately there was no fire and no-one was hurt in the crash. We clambered out and on the way I found the navigator dead. It was an American airfield and they got to work on our wounds straight away.'

The citation for Flt Lt Reid read: 'The Victoria Cross has been awarded to a bomber pilot who, wounded in two attacks, without oxygen, suffering severely from cold, his navigator dead, his wireless operator fatally wounded and his aircraft crippled and defenceless, went on to bomb his target – Dusseldorf.' It continued that the Conspicious Gallantry Medal had also been awarded to Sgt J Norris, the flight engineer. Flt Lt Reid was just one of seventeen members of the RAF to be awarded a VC and it was one that Syerston was justly proud of.

No 106 Squadron were now due to leave the airfield. On 11th November, they moved to Metheringham, Norfolk, there to remain until the end of the war. Devoid of bomber squadrons, Syerston ceased to be an operational station. There followed a succession of training units, beginning with No 1485 Bombing and Gunnery Flight in late November. Equipped with Wellingtons and Martinets, the latter an aircraft designed and built as a target-tug, they towed banners and various other targets for fighter aircraft to practise gunnery. No 1668 Heavy Conversion Unit arrived a few weeks later equipped with eighteen Lancasters. Once again the sound of four-engined bombers reverberated around the locality. With the push to victory, the HCU was renamed No 5 Lancaster Finishing School. The penultimate year of war saw No 1690 Bomber Defence

Training Flight form at Syerston before moving to Scampton, whilst No 1485 B&G Flight was disbanded. The Lancaster Finishing School disbanded in March 1945, but in April Syerston once again became an operational station with the arrival of No 49 Squadron from Fulbeck. Flying the Lancaster I and II, they carried out one bombing mission to Berchtesgaden on 25th April, the last to be mounted from Syerston.

Victory saw the airfield transfer from No 5 Group Bomber Command to No 4 Group Training Command on 20th October 1945. It continued as a flying station with a variety of aircraft using its facilities. No 504 (County of Nottingham) Squadron, R.AuxAF reformed at Syerston with Mosquitos before moving to the permanent base at Hucknall a year later. By 1948 Syerston had become the home of No 22 Flying Training School before the school was renumbered No 2 FTS. In 1958 this unit acquired the then new Hunting Jet Provost trainer, putting Syerston once again in the history books as the first RAF station in the world to train student pilots on jet aircraft.

Yet even in peacetime the airfield was to see tragedy. On 20th September 1958, the station hosted an annual Battle of Britain Airshow. In front of thousands of the public who had come to see

Disaster struck at Syerston when a Vulcan, similar to the one seen here, exploded in mid-air. (Author)

153

the peacetime air force in action, an Avro Vulcan, the second of the V bombers to be in service, broke up in mid-air killing its entire crew. It was a sad, vivid reminder that tragedy was never far away.

When No 2 FTS left, Syerston went into Care and Maintenance. It was revived in 1976 when the RAF Central Gliding School arrived to give Air Cadets air experience and instruction in maintaining their aircraft, with Newton as the parent station.

Syerston has had many of its permanent buildings, demolished but the hangar and airfield are busy virtually every day of the year with modern Air Cadet gliders.

16

TOLLERTON

National Grid Reference SK620360, 3 miles SE of Nottingham

By 1928, Air Vice-Marshal Sir Sefton Brancker had become the director of civil aviation. His one ambition was to make British aviation a world leader, his first big achievement being the flights of the R.100 and R.101 Airships. He saw the airship as the key to Britain's future prosperity and applied pressure to many quarters and organisations to make his dream come true. This pressure was to be applied to the hastily built R.101, which Brancker hoped would demonstrate to the world that Britain was indeed a leader. Convinced that the airship was the key, Brancker decided that he should go on the maiden flight to India.

By the morning of 4th October 1930, the R.101 was deemed ready to depart and throughout the day the VIP passengers arrived. It was a wet, squally day but by nightfall it was felt, given that there had been a slight improvement in the weather, that no further delay could be afforded. At 19.34 hours, the airship slipped from her bondage at Cardington in Bedfordshire and pointed her nose for London and the English Channel. The great journey had begun. All went well until the R.101 was a few miles from Beauvais in France. In a storm that the crew had known about but had been told to disregard, the great airship crashed at 02.30 hours and burst into flames. There were only six survivors; the rest perished in the conflagration, including Sir Sefton Brancker.

Earlier that year on 19th June, Sefton Brancker had officially opened Tollerton airfield. Originally just a big field outside the

155

village of Tollerton, a licence to use it for flying was granted to Nottingham Corporation on 27th July 1929. They in turn leased it to National Flying Services, who erected a clubhouse and hangar in a corner of the field. It became a social hot-spot, well known for its staff's culinary expertise. Weekends would see light aircraft abound on the grass whilst passengers enjoyed the facilities on offer.

On 12th May 1932, Alan Cobham's National Aviation Day Display visited Tollerton. It attracted a crowd of several hundred, some eager to get airborne on five-shilling (25p) trips. It returned on 4th June 1933, this time cramming several thousand of the public into the little airfield. The attractions were a three engined biplane called a Ferry, several De Havilland Moths, the faithful Avro 504K, a Comper Swift, a Southern Martlet and a Cierva Autogiro. Admission was one shilling and sixpence (7½p) and with this came a programme detailing the events and aircraft. Such was the attraction that it came back in 1934 and 1935. Alan Cobham, in bringing aviation to the attention of the masses, also entertained Council officials in the hope that they would set up a municipal airport. In the case of Tollerton, his influence certainly worked as the council renamed the airfield Nottingham Airport.

Nottingham Flying Club moved their organisation from Hucknall to the airfield in September 1931. A Flight and Test Establishment was set up at the same time calling itself the Hucknall Flight and Test Company. Growing in size each year, they looked for larger premises and found room at Hucknall, moving there in December 1934. The airfield now firmly on the aviation map, it came to the attention of an organisation known as Railway Air Services.

In 1931 there was only one regular air service within the UK, a twice daily flight between Skegness and Hunstanton, a distance of 19 miles. As better and larger passenger carrying aircraft were produced, further companies set up domestic air services. One of the new players was a combination of the British Mainline Railways and Imperial Airways, which eventually became Railway Air Services. It was they who developed many trunk air routes linking cities within the British Isles. One such route, set up on 27th May 1935, was the west of England route with its northern terminal at Nottingham. It worked via Birmingham, Cardiff and Denbury to terminate at Plymouth, using two De Havilland Dragon aircraft. The service was to prove very

Aircraft of Nottingham Flying Club and National Flying Services parked in front of the clubhouse, circa 1937/8. (Harper Shaw via Derek Leatherland)

popular and only ended when war was declared. However, in 1940 certain services had re-opened to finally close in 1947.

With the airfield now fully established, the Nottingham Flying Club continued to expand. During 1934, National Flying Services vacated the field and the lease was taken up by the Chief Flying Instructor of the club, Captain L W Hall. This allowed the Nottingham Flying Club to continue, but with the rumblings of war, the club was asked to set up a branch of the Civil Air Guard. Immediately, fifty people applied to take up the flying training. The CAG was joined by No 27 E&RFTS, which formed on 24th June 1938. Run on military lines, it contrasted with the CAG, which was more lenient. Open to both sexes, the CAG anticipated pupils gaining their 'A' Licence after 10 to 11 hours' dual training. This was usually accomplished in De Havilland 60G Moths whereas the E&RFTS had an assortment of aircraft including Miles Magisters, Avro Ansons and Hawker Harts. However, when war did come, both organisations played their part in providing front line pilots.

Rapid expansion took place during 1938. A large factory hangar was built on the west side of the airfield and occupied by Field Aircraft Services Ltd, an aviation engineering company based at Croydon Airport in Surrey. They were eventually to run a repair and servicing organisation at Nottingham Airport in support of the military.

On 3rd September 1939, all civil flying at the airfield ceased and Nottingham Airport, requisitioned by the Air Ministry, became RAF Tollerton. It was not immediately used operationally, but as a relief field for two Waddington-based Hampden squadrons, Nos 44 and 50. Field Aircraft Services were allowed to continue their work whilst Tollerton was deemed a satellite to Newton.

The Battle of Britain saw no action for the airfield despite a heavy raid on the city on the night of 7th September 1940. Still a grass airfield, plans were formulated to lay three runways, two 1,120 yards long and one 1,000 yards long. Further hangars were built, together with other buildings, with the entire expansion taking until 1941. The very limited use of Tollerton began when No 16 (Polish) SFTS based at Newton used the airfield to practise take-offs and landings. Over on the west side, Field Aircraft

An unusual photo of a damaged Battle of 103 Squadron. It is pictured at Tollerton, after colliding with Battle K9373 on 6th August 1939. The code letters (GV) do not apply to 103 Squadron whose code was PM, but to No 1652 conversion unit who did not fly Battles. This is something of a mystery. (via Andy Thomas)

Services were busy repairing and overhauling mainly bomber aircraft such as Lancasters, Hampdens, Halifaxes and Dakotas. With the military expressing very little interest in the airfield as a base for squadrons, this turned out to be the main work connected with the war effort at Tollerton. Ferried by the men and women of the Air Transport Auxiliary, the aircraft were flown back to the squadrons when they were ready to resume operations.

Very little changed throughout the rest of the war. With victory in 1945, it was estimated that Field Aircraft Services had completed 1,700 aircraft for the Ministry of Aircraft Production plus 2,000 components. Their last job for the war effort was to scrap large numbers of Lancasters then deemed to be surplus to requirements. (If only foresight had prevailed and some had been saved!) In 1947 the Nottingham Flying Club reformed and the Ministry of Aviation allowed civilian airlines to begin scheduled services, hoping that Tollerton would once again become the airport for Nottingham. The airlines did not last long and in 1949, the Ministry gave up the lease. The flying club

A superb aerial view of Tollerton taken around 1942. It shows a typical bomber station layout, though Tollerton was not used in this role. (Harper Shaw via Derek Leatherland)

The main hangar filled with aircraft types under repair by Field Aircraft Services. (Harper Shaw via Derek Leatherland)

Polish airmen of No 16 (Polish) SFTS with a Harvard pictured at the RLG of Tollerton circa 1944/5. (RR Heritage Trust via David Birch)

closed down although visiting aircraft still used the site. It became a satellite for No 22 FTS at Syerston, carrying this role through to 1956 when the Air Ministry found no further use for Tollerton. Field Aircraft Services remained until 1957, when they moved out to Wymeswold. The airfield remained neglected until 1963, when Truman Aviation took over on a 75-year lease. Once again it became a hub for private aviation and remains that way today, still managed by Truman Aviation.

Tollerton was not used to its full potential during wartime, yet it survives as an executive and private airfield and is still in business as Nottingham Airport.

17

WIGSLEY

National Grid Reference SK8555695, 7 miles W of Lincoln

When war was declared on 3rd September 1939 and our need was greatest, the Commonwealth of Nations rose to help in the conquest of the enemy. The air forces of those countries, steeped in their own traditions, crossed continents to give their all in conquering the Nazi tyranny. One of those countries was Australia. As the Commonwealth forces mobilised, the first unit to come to Great Britain from Australia was No 10 Squadron, equipped with Sunderland Flying Boats. Prior to this, Australia had helped the mother country when the Australian government assisted with the Empire Air Training Scheme. This alone provided 50,000 trained aircrew each year. Of the thirty Australians that flew in the Battle of Britain, fifteen were killed in action. They were in every major operation mounted by Bomber Command, one of the squadrons being No 455, which arrived at Wigsley on 8th February 1942.

Situated between the villages of Wigsley and Spalford, the airfield was a late-comer to the war, finally opening in February 1942 as a satellite to Swinderby. Encompassed within No 5 Group Bomber Command, it was built to a standard bomber layout. Once completed, No 455 Squadron, having formed at Swinderby, flew their Handley Page Hampdens in on 8th February. By this period of the war, the Hampden's days as a front-line bomber were past, yet they were still used for minor operations. Several of these were carried out by the squadron, mainly on the German held French ports. In addition, nickelling operations, the dropping of leaflets over enemy territory, were still being carried out.

Part of the Government's propaganda campaign, the nickelling provided an excellent and unique method of continuing training. For the Australian crews, who had received very little training on arrival, this sometimes called for greater endurance than did bombing raids. Dropped through the flare-chute, which was specially adapted for the purpose, the leaflets were packed in bundles secured by a piece of string, which was cut before the bundle was pushed down the chute. Once entering the slip-stream, the leaflets were blown far and wide. Though No 455 continued to use their Hampdens in this role, the type was also undergoing trials with the Torpedo Development Unit at Gosport in Hampshire. With the trials proving that the aircraft could be employed successfully as a torpedo bomber, three squadrons, including No 455, were detached from No 5 Group for anti-shipping operations. This, however, entailed a move and on 28th April 1942, No 455 squadron moved to Leuchars in Scotland to carry out anti-shipping operations as part of Coastal Command.

There was also a change of role for Wigsley as No 1654 HCU arrived from Swinderby in June 1942. Once again the unit consisted of Manchesters and Lancasters, which were used to further the training of aircrew personnel direct from the OTUs. Wigsley was steadily becoming a very busy station as, day and night, the two-engined Manchesters and the four-engined Lancasters became a familiar sight and sound around the area. It may have been this intense activity that attracted the first attack on the airfield. With a low cloud base and occasional rain, 3rd July 1942 saw two Ju88s flying at low level to approach the airfield from the east. They fired at a Manchester at dispersal, causing slight damage, but it is assumed that they had already dropped their bombs on another target. In only a few seconds, the enemy aircraft made for the safety of the low cloud without the airfield defence gunners having time to fire.

Intense activity continued as a night-flying programme was introduced. On 23rd July, one of the exercises consisted of local and cross-country flights. The exercise completed, the aircraft prepared to land back at Wigsley. Lancaster R5801 overshot on the landing and came to rest in a ditch adjoining the perimeter track, damaging its undercarriage and front fuselage but luckily

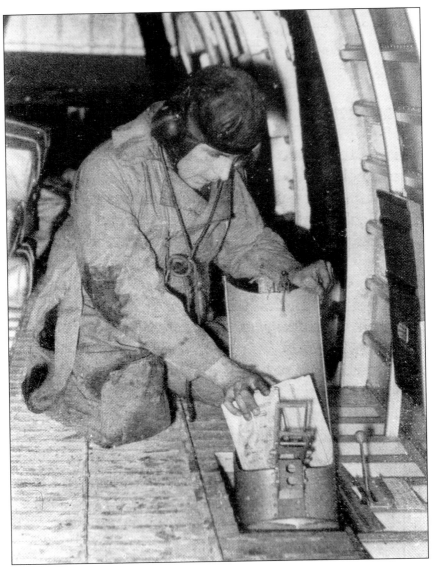

'Nickelling' – the leaflets are pushed through the flare chute. (Crown)

Place	Date	Time	Summary of Events SECRET.	References to Appendices
WIGSLEY.	28 Dec.	(cont'd)	FLYING TRAINING. DAY. Nil, owing to poor visibility.	
			NIGHT. 2 crews took part in a night-fighter and searchlight co-operation exercise, another completed a cross-country exercise which included Time and Distance runs and Infra Red bombing, whilst 3 crews practised circuits and landings.	
			FLYING TIMES. DAY. Nil. NIGHT. 17 hours, 25 minutes.	
			ENTERTAINMENT. A W.A.A.F. Carnival Dance took place in the W.A.A.F. N.A.A.F.I. commencing at 20.00 hours. The Station Band provided music for Dancing and refreshments were available, resulting in a very pleasant evening for a very large attendance.	
	29 Dec.		WEATHER. Fair to fine, with slight haze. Moderate visibility. South Westerly wind, veering North Westerly later.	
			TRAINING. Course 27 - Flying Instruction.	
			Course 50 - Day - 20 - Flying Instruction.	
			FLYING TRAINING. DAY. 5 crews took part in a Fighter Affiliation Exercise. 1 crew completed a short cross country with bombing and Air/Sea firing, followed by a climb and landing with full load. 2 crews completed short cross country flights and a further 9 crews practised circuits and landings on Stirling aircraft.	
			NIGHT. 5 crews took part in a Local Bullseye Exercise, which included searchlight and fighter co-operation. 2 crews completed a short cross country, including practice bombing, Time and Distance runs and Infra Red bombing, while a further 5 crews practised circuits and landings on Stirling aircraft.	
			FLYING TIMES. DAY. 37 hours, 40 minutes. NIGHT. 35 hours, 15 minutes.	
			ENTERTAINMENT. A Concert, given by The Vagabonds, Skellingthorpe Concert Party, was enjoyed by a full house in the Station Cinema.	

The Wigsley ORB stating a hectic training schedule. (PRO-Air 28/487)

with no casualties. Later, on the 13th, seven crews were detailed to carry out an operation against Bremen. With the aircraft taking off between 23.09 hours and 23.37 hours, six Lancasters found the target and successfully bombed, but one, piloted by Plt Off Dondell, failed to return.

The new year saw Wigsley performing the same role, retaining its satellite classification when, in March 1943, Swinderby changed its title to No 51 Base. Many of the training operations carried out by the unit went under the name of 'Bullseye'. It was on such an operation that Lancaster 'O' flown by Sgt Bryde crashed at Humbleton, three miles north east of Hull. Sadly, the entire crew perished. As the Manchesters were phased out due to their lack of performance and the unreliability of their engines, the Lancasters were also taken for front-line bombing operations. This forced No 1654 HCU to convert to the Short Stirling III. Relegated from major operations with Bomber Command, the Stirling was put to other uses including the training of four-engined aircrew. For the next year they flew from Wigsley as the airfield became No 75 Base in No 7 Group.

The Short Stirling, workhorse of many HCUs. (Shorts)

With the end of the war looming, the need for heavy bomber pilots dwindled, with No 1654 HCU moving to Woolfox Lodge on 20th September 1945. Wigsley became No 28 Aircrew Holding Unit, only to see the unit disband a year later. It remained open as a satellite for the flying training schools at Swinderby, seeing intensive flying until 1st July 1958, when the airfield was de-requisitioned and returned to agriculture. For many years afterwards the control tower languished as a sentinel, used by the local farmer for storage. Nature took over most of the buildings and today very little remains to remind us of this airfield.

18

WINTHORPE

National Grid Reference SK825565, 1½ miles NE of Newark

In 1948, a monument was erected on the NE corner of Northolt aerodrome in Middlesex to the memory of Polish pilots who had lost their lives flying from the airfield during the Second World War (see *Thames Valley Airfields in the Second World War*). Erected out of funds contributed by members of the Polish Armed Forces and the general public, the unveiling ceremony on 2nd November 1948 was the culmination of an idea that had its origins back in 1943. The day was attended by the then president of the Polish Republic, M. August Zaleski, various British government officials, members of the British, American and Polish Forces and the public. It fell to Marshal of the Royal Air Force, Viscount Portal, Lord Tedder, to unveil the memorial, after which the Reverend Gogolinski paid tribute to all the Polish airmen killed whilst flying from Northolt. A similar memorial was erected at Newark commemorating some of the Polish airmen who had lost their lives whilst flying from Winthorpe, one of the Nottinghamshire airfields that was to play host to Polish squadrons.

Situated NE of Newark between the villages of Winthorpe and Coddington, Winthorpe was one of the bomber airfields built during the expansion period of the late 1930s. It was a typical three runway bomber layout with a communal site and workshop area. Designated a satellite for nearby Swinderby, it

Winthorpe Station Headquarters (SSQ) during 1945. (W.Taylor)

officially opened in September 1940 and was intended to be used by Nos 300 (Ziemi Mazowieckiej – Land of Mazovia) and 301 (Ziemi Pomorskiej Obroncow Warszawy – Land of Pomerania Warsaw Defenders) Polish bomber squadrons. Both squadrons were based at Swinderby in late August 1940 and initially used Winthorpe as a satellite. They had formed at Bramcote in July 1940 as part of Bomber Command together with two other Polish units, Nos 304 (Slaskiej) and 305 (Wielkopolska). Each squadron flew the Fairey Battle light bomber, one of the key types chosen by the Air Ministry for the rapidly expanding RAF during the late 1930s, but one that had become obsolete by the time the war began. Designed to meet the requirements of Air Ministry Spec P.27/32 issued in April 1933, it was a single-engined monoplane of all metal, stressed skin construction and powered by a single 1,030hp Rolls-Royce Merlin 1 engine. Despite the Merlin, the aircraft proved to be under-powered and lacked both speed and defensive fire-power. With one Browning gun forward and one Vickers 'R' gun aft, it was no match for the superior aircraft flown by the Luftwaffe. The outbreak of war in 1939 saw the Battles of No 226 Squadron sent to France to form the spearhead of the

Advanced Air Striking Force. This and other squadrons suffered badly at the hands of the enemy and by the time the Polish squadrons had formed at Bramcote, the type had been relegated to a training role.

For No 300 the move to Swinderby came on 22 August 1940, No 301 moving in seven days later. Training immediately got underway with instruction in night flying, formation flying and bombing and navigation exercises. One problem encountered with the Polish airmen was their lack of basic English. Since their arrival in Britain, crash courses in the language had taken place. In order to lessen the problem, a British officer was appointed to understudy the Polish commanders. No 300 Squadron was commanded by 2nd Colonel Wacklaw Makowsli with Sqn Ldr C G Skinner of the RAF as his adviser. He was also to be the adviser to the CO of No 301 Squadron, 2nd Colonel Roman Rudlowski, and whilst in the beginning the task proved rather ponderous, the Poles very soon took the English language to heart and were quick learners.

With good progress in the training at both airfields, the night of 14th/15th September 1940 saw the first operational bomber raid by the Poles. Three aircraft from each squadron were airborne at 18.23 hours to attack the invasion barges sitting in Boulogne Harbour. All aircraft returned safely but a similar raid on 13th October, whilst successful, found on the return trip that the weather had changed dramatically, causing navigational problems. In addition, and assisted by a waxing moon, enemy aircraft roaming across the Midlands had found and infiltrated the Swinderby circuit. In order to confuse these raiders, the airfield lights had been switched off, making the task for the Poles even more difficult. All the Battles were by then low on fuel and with all three crew members in each aircraft desperately looking for a flat area in which to crash-land, two aircraft from No 300 came to grief. L5499 (BH-Y), with crew members, Fg Off Jan Gebicki (pilot), Sgt Edward Morana (observer) and Sgt Tadeusz Egierski (air gunner), crashed at Watchwood Plantation at Blidworth around 23.30 hours. Tragically, all the crew perished. The cause was put down to loss of control after five hours flying in difficult conditions. A second Battle, L5427 (BH-K), also crashed on its return from Boulogne at Sherwood with the crew, Fg Off Szponarowicz, Sgt Koczwarski and Sgt Sztun, escaping with minor injuries.

These raids were but a few of many similar ones taking place around this period of the war. It is true that Hitler did not want war with Britain; he would far rather have negotiated a peaceful, diplomatic solution. But his army and Luftwaffe had successfully overrun the countries of Europe and now they were poised at the Channel coast. In the SE corner of England, the Battle of Britain had been fought and won by the RAF despite the assurances of the Commander-in-Chief of the Luftwaffe, Hermann Goering, that the skies above Kent and Sussex would be cleared of the RAF. They were not and, with Britain refusing to negotiate terms, plans had been drawn up for an invasion in the autumn of 1940. The preparation included the siting of barges and small ships in the many German held French ports along the Pas-de-Calais. It was these that the Polish squadrons, together with others, had been detailed to attack. Operation 'Sealion', Hitler's planned offensive against Britain was set for 15th September 1940, yet still the Luftwaffe did not have control of the skies and with the autumn storms setting in, it was decided to abandon the invasion until the coming spring. At the time, however, with this very real threat, both Polish squadrons were active attacking the usual targets of the barges in Boulogne, Calais, Dunkirk and Ostend. The Luftwaffe meanwhile were moving their attacks on Britain far inland.

Monday 14th October was a day of widespread small enemy attacks. With occasional rain or drizzle in the Channel and cloud in the North Sea, it was 10.15 am before the Germans got together a formation and head towards the English coastline. They damaged London and the south east towns but it was the raids that took place between 23.00 hours and 01.00 hours that managed to reach the Nottinghamshire area. One particular raid found Swinderby and dropped ten bombs on the runway, damaging two aircraft, whilst another raider found Winthorpe and dropped a parachute mine. The duty personnel had seen the parachute open as the enemy flew across and drew the obvious conclusion that it was a parachutist. Bringing their guns to the ready, they suddenly saw that it was a mine hanging on the end and promptly ran to a shelter. The ensuing explosion made an enormous crater in the grass landing area but no loss of life was incurred.

With the squadron struggling on with the obsolete Battles, news filtered through that they were soon to receive the

Wellington bomber. The backbone of Bomber Command at that time, the design was noteworthy due to the fact that it could withstand a lot of punishment. Known as the geodetic construction, it was a metal strip structure which was fabric covered. Designed by Barnes Wallis, the prototype (K4049) first flew on 15th June 1936. The Mark 1s which the squadrons were to receive were powered by two 1,000hp Bristol Pegasus XVIII engines. Two of the aircraft flew into Winthorpe in October 1940 for No 301 Squadron.

The losses, however, were still continuing with the Battles, one incident, on 29th October, proving particularly bad. Whilst on a training flight, Battle L5356 lost a port wing in a dive and crashed into an orchard at Sutton-on-Trent. Sadly the crew of three, G Toebel, S Firlei Bielanski and T J Smajdowicz, all perished and were laid to rest in the Polish cemetery at Newark. That the squadron did valuable work with these obsolete aircraft can be seen by the statistics. From 15th September to 18th October, they dropped more than 45 tons of bombs during 85 operations. Now with the newer aircraft arriving, both squadrons looked forward to even better results.

With the approach of Christmas 1940, thoughts turned to a few days without operations. With the Battle of Britain over in the south of the country, the enemy had turned his attention to bombing London. This had little effect on the Midlands and a traditional Polish Christmas was enjoyed by both units, although everyone wondered just what 1941 would bring. The weather around January was particularly atrocious and was the cause of many incidents.

The night of 13th/14th January saw both squadrons detailed to attack Bremen. With the groundcrews preparing the aircraft during the afternoon, a briefing was held behind sealed doors. Details of the target, weather conditions over Europe and bomb and fuel loads were given before the aircrews boarded the trucks to take them to the waiting Wellingtons. By this time, No 300 Squadron had converted to the type, glad to leave their old Battles behind. They encountered very changeable weather on the outbound journey but, having dropped their bombs successfully, the return was to prove far worse. Frequent snow showers with very low cloud causing severe icing conditions hampered the crews as they crossed the coast and looked for their home base. First to attempt a landing was a Wellington from

301 Squadron. Coming in low over the threshold, the pilot made a heavy landing causing the undercarriage to collapse. With this the landing area was obstructed and radio messages were sent to the remaining aircraft to divert to other airfields. This caused problems and, sadly, another two 301 Wellingtons crashed on the approach to Digby airfield. In this carnage, only one rear gunner survived.

The bad weather rendered Swinderby unserviceable during January and all training was concentrated on Winthorpe. Over this period the aircraft flew to Newton and Syerston for bombing up and carrying out further raids on Germany. Targets included the Ruhr Valley, Dusseldorf and, of course, Bremen. February and March continued to be bad months with several losses of aircraft and crews. One particular loss was on 21st March, when Wellington L7874 of 301 Squadron approached the threshold too high. Realising his mistake, the pilot, Sgt Lenczowski, attempted to overshoot on full power but the aircraft stalled and crashed about two miles from the airfield. Tragically, the pilot Fg Off Korycinski (observer) and Sgt Chrzanowski (observer/gunner) were all killed. Like many other Polish airmen, they were laid to rest in Newark cemetery.

The new few months were spent in similar vein but with plans for a big expansion programme at Winthorpe, the days of the Polish squadrons there were numbered. In early July a signal was received that both Nos 300 and 301 were to relocate to Hemswell. Before this, however, the month also saw many of the original Polish airmen complete their operational tour and take on instructional flying. At a parade and service for all the Polish bomber squadrons held at Newark cemetery on 14th July 1941, a granite cross was unveiled along with the reading of the names of all the dead and missing aircrew. Two days later No 300 Squadron was presented with the Polish Air Force Standard, which was held for three months before passing on to other Polish units. This final gesture was very apt for on 18th July both squadrons moved to Hemswell never to return to Winthorpe.

With their departure, control of the station passed to Ossington. From this period until the beginning of 1942, very little use was made of the airfield. There was a brief acquaintance with No 455 Squadron of Coastal Command in the autumn, when it was used in the disposal role for their Handley Page Hampden bombers. Having reformed at Swinderby on 6th June

The magnificent Polish war memorial at Newark-on-Trent cemetery.
(B. Clements)

1941, an echelon was sent to Williamstown in Australia but arrived back in the UK in September. The squadron were mainly employed on attacking German shipping in the North Sea and were later to operate from bases in Russia. By February 1942 they had moved to Wigsley and the use of Winthorpe ceased.

Immediately, a period of intense reconstruction began at the airfield, including the building of hard runways. Designed to the standard bomber layout of the period, the main runway was 2,000 yards long with two intersecting runways of 1,430 yards. Despite the expansions, 1942 saw very little use of Winthorpe. It was returned to the control of Swinderby as a second satellite on 15th October as a new use for the airfield became evident. Accordingly, on 1st January 1943, No 1661 Heavy Conversion Unit (HCU) was established. Part of No 5 Group of Bomber Command, the unit had formed at Waddington on 7th October 1942 with Sqn Ldr J Nettleton VC as its first Commanding Officer. It operated a combination of Avro aircraft, the Manchester and the Lancaster, in a training role, the object of which was to train OTU pilots and co-pilots to fly both types of aircraft before being posted to operational squadrons. No 1661 was formed as the result of amalgamating Nos 9, 44 and 49 Bomber Squadron Conversion Units and upon its arrival at Winthorpe was commanded by Wg Cdr Beauchamp DSO, DFC. The complement of aircraft were 'A' Flight operating eight Manchesters, 'B' Flight five Lancasters and 'C' Flight five Lancasters.

It had fallen to 'A' Flight to operate one of the RAF's great disappointments of the war. The Avro Manchester was a failure on operations and became very unpopular with its crews. This, however, was no fault of the basic aircraft design but rather of the installation of unreliable engines. Though of Rolls-Royce design, the Vulture failed to deliver its expected power, resulting in many losses both in aircraft and crews. Production ceased in November 1941 after 200 had been built, a long way short of its expected run. The training syllabus at Winthorpe was six weeks in length, half of which was spent on the Manchester and half on the Lancaster. It became well known that each crew was glad to move on to the latter.

With the heavier aircraft, and despite the fact that the airfield now had hard runways, moving from dispersal onto the runway was still to prove a problem as the ground that had to be crossed was of a soft

An aerial view of Winthorpe taken in 1945. (via W. Taylor)

nature. Wheels were prone to sink into the grass, especially after a period of intense rain. Much heaving and puffing by groundcrews and pulling by tractors seemed to go on for a considerable time!

With the war now seemingly going the way of the Allies, Bomber Command was pushed to its limit to keep up the relentless attacks on German cities. Churchill had said in one of his war cabinet minutes: 'The navy can lose us the war but only the air force can win it. The fighters are our salvation but the bombers alone can provide the means of victory.' The first attacks on Berlin came in response to the bombing attacks on London. On 24th August 1940, a force of 81 Whitleys, Wellingtons and Hampdens set out for the capital. Unfortunately the weather over Berlin was not as predicted and thick layers of cloud partly obscured the target. Out of the force, only twenty-nine reported seeing their bombs hit the city, but this was just the first of many raids to be unleashed on Berlin. Between August 1940 and November 1941, Bomber Command attacked on more than fifty occasions. Now, in 1943, even more effort was to be placed upon destroying the German capital.

Although a conversion unit, No 1661 HCU was also to play a part in 'Operations Target Berlin'. The night of 16th January 1943

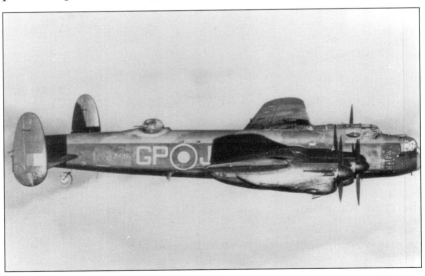

A fine air-to-air photo of a Lancaster I (W4113-GP-J) flying from Winthorpe. (A. Thomas)

A Manchester of No 1661 HCU in one of the Winthorpe dispersals.
(via W. Taylor)

saw 1661 HCU brief the crews of five Lancasters for an attack on Berlin, known to all aircrew as the 'Big City'. This was the first time the unit had been scheduled to join a bomber force from 5 Group and the resulting problems were indicative of just how unprepared at this stage of the war the HCUs were to carry out such attacks. Lancaster W4271 was airborne at 17.13 hours, 30 minutes later than 5 Group had scheduled. On reaching the Dutch coast the pilot, Flt Lt Gunter, decided that he would be late over the target, a very dangerous position to be in, and so returned to base at 22.15 hours. Lancaster W4123 was also not ready on time and so failed to take off at all, whilst Lancaster R5904 went unserviceable due to a faulty mid-upper turret. Only Lancaster W4258 made it to the target. Airborne at 17.07 hours, the crew found intense flak over the city. They dropped their bombs, but the photo-flash misfunctioned and so no photos of the target could be taken. Plt Off Fletcher landed back at Winthorpe at 00.24 hours to find that the other Lancaster, R5842, had failed to get airborne. The next night was more successful, with all five Lancasters reaching Berlin and returning safely. This raid was unique due to the fact that R5842 had the first encounter

The ground crew of 'C' Flight, No 1661 HCU pose in front of a Lancaster at Winthorpe during 1942. (via W. Taylor)

with an enemy night-fighter. Airborne at 16.42 hours, before reaching the coast of Denmark a twin-engined night-fighter, possibly an Me110, approached the Lancaster three times. Taking evasive action, Plt Off Hartley managed to lose the enemy in cloud. Approaching the target area, bombs were dropped at 20.47 hours from 18,000 feet amidst heavy flak. The return journey proved uneventful and on landing back at Winthorpe a hole caused by flak was discovered in the fuselage.

The next few months were played out in similar vein. On 23rd May 1943, a section of No 1661 HCU took part in the 'Wings of Victory' parade in the village of Winthorpe and in the open air service held in the market place. Six days later No 4808 Airfield Construction Flight arrived to carry out work on reconstructing the perimeter track in the hope of preventing the aircraft sinking into the ground. The unit was able to carry on flying whilst this essential work was carried out but in September, due to repair work on the main runway, the aircraft and a contingent of groundcrews moved over to Balderton to continue conversion

Taken from the pilot's position, the photo shows a Lancaster of No 1661 HCU taking off from Winthorpe. (W. Taylor)

training. At the same time, Gp Cpt N C Pleasance was posted in from HQ No 39 Group to take over command of Winthorpe.

A change also took place in the airfield defence when the regular unit, No 2776 Squadron of the RAF Regiment, were sent on an AA course, to be replaced by No 2772 Squadron. Though airfield defence was originally a task for the army, the RAF Regiment was formed on 1st February 1942 initially under the command of Major-General Liardet. They took over the defence tasks almost immediately, a duty that continues today.

As summer 1943 progressed, Winston Churchill ordered the RAF to continue and intensify the bombing campaign. The constant bombing of the industrial Ruhr Valley and Rhineland had prompted the Nazi government to declare the areas war zones. A mass evacuation of Berlin and the major cities was underway, a situation that was exacerbated by approval being given to the American 8th Air Force to commence daylight raids. The intensification of raids placed a further demand on the OTUs and HCUs for more aircrew. This in turn meant that further accidents were inevitable and to illustrate the dangers that the conversion crews faced when not even over enemy territory, an incident that happened on 16th December 1943 is indicative of many other tragedies.

Lancaster LM307 was airborne on a training flight during the early evening of the sixteenth. At 20.15 hours, and without prior warning, it dived and crashed one mile north of South Muskham, Nottinghamshire. Due to the nature and severity of the ensuing fire, Plt Off Eager (pilot/instructor), Flt Sgt Hampson (pilot), Sgt Lawrence (flight engineer), Sgt Austin (navigator), Sgt Woolcock (WOp/air gunner) and Flt Sgt Baldwin (bomb airman) were killed outright. Sgt Dillon (air gunner) and Sgt East (air gunner) were transferred to Newark General Hospital with severe burns and shock. At 6 am the next day, Sgt Dillon died from his injuries. This is just one fatal and sad incident of many that occurred during the training of bomber crews.

In the late autumn of 1943, sixteen Handley Page Halifax bombers arrived at the HCU. The second of Britain's four-engined bombers to enter service with the RAF, it was actually preceded into squadron service by the four-engined Short Stirling. Their arrival at Winthorpe brought about the end of the Manchesters, something that was not regretted by 1661 HCU.

A rare photo of a No 1661 HCU Stirling landing at Winthorpe.
(via W. Taylor)

They had only been used on familiarity flights due to their unreliability and poor performance. The Halifaxes, however, did not remain long as, like the Lancasters, they were needed for Bomber Command. In their place came the Short Stirling, the first four-engined monoplane bomber to enter service and the first to be used operationally. Though it carried out many bombing raids during the early war years, it was soon superseded by the Halifax and Lancaster and had been relegated to lesser uses such as conversion units and usage as a tug. Like the Manchester, the Stirling had several vices, amongst which was a greater fire risk and difficult handling. Once again, 1661 was to suffer many accidents and losses.

As 1944 dawned, Gp Cpt Pleasance was posted to RAF Bardney to be succeeded by Gp Cpt E L S Ward DFC. Lieutenant-General Carl Spaatz took command of the US Strategic Air Forces in Europe and took over the responsibility for all American long-range bombing of Germany as the final push to victory began.

For Gp Cpt Ward, command of Winthorpe came at a very difficult time. The Stirlings were proving not to be the best type to convert pilots to four-engined aircraft, as the ORB for the station relates. On 21st January 1944, Stirling EF151 lost one of its engines after a training sortie lasting three hours. Attempting to land back at Winthorpe, and with the undercarriage only partly down, the aircraft hit some trees on its final approach and crashed at Glebe Farm, Brough, Newark. It immediately burst into flames. Of the crew, the pilot, Sgt Docherty, was admitted to the SSQ and then transferred to RAF Hospital Rauceby, Sgt Venables (flight eng) was admitted to Newark Hospital but died later from his wounds, Flt Sgt Munro (navigator) and Sgt Cooper (WOp/air gunner) both died instantly, whilst Sgt Biddle (bomb aimer), Sgt Southey (air gunner) and Sgt Humphreys (air gunner) were admitted to the SSQ. Just to illustrate that this was not an isolated incident, on the night of 26th February, Stirling EF127 was returning to base after a night training sortie. Running short of fuel, the navigator sent a 'Mayday' signal which was received at RAF Syerston. An attempt was made to contact the Stirling without success and minutes later the aircraft struck some trees and crashed at approximately 01.30 hours. Wreckage was thrown over three fields at Alby's Farm near Edwinstowe, Nottinghamshire. Tragically, five members of the crew, Flt Sgt W V Manuel (pilot), Sgt G Davison (Flt/Eng), Flt Sgt G D Bird (navigator), Sgt Macoun (bomb aimer) and Flt Sgt S E Christie (W/op air gunner) were killed instantly. Flt Sgt R Plath (air gunner) and Sgt W Taylor (air gunner) suffered injuries and were admitted to hospital.

Late February saw heavy snowfall within the region and all ranks were put to the arduous task of snow clearance. This caused many problems with several Stirlings managing to become embedded in some of the snow banks alongside the runway. By March the weather had improved enough to allow a new unit to arrive at Winthorpe. A detachment of No 1690 (Bomber Defence Training Flight) under the command of Flt Lt Baker brought their three Miles Martinet aircraft into the base. Built by Miles Aircraft Ltd at Woodley airfield near Reading, it was the first aircraft to enter RAF service which had been designed purely as a target tug. In this role it had proved a great success with 1,724 aircraft being built between 1942 and 1945. They remained at Winthorpe until July, when they returned to Scampton.

On 27th April, Gp Cpt J H Woodin arrived to replace Gp Cpt Ward as station commander. One of his first duties was to officiate at the opening of the 'Salute the Soldier Week'. Both men and women from Winthorpe took part in a march-past, church service and parade during the week, in which over £500 was raised towards the local area target of £25,000.

Operation 'Overload', the allied invasion of Europe, came on 6th June 1944. Though it had little effect on the day to day operations of Winthorpe, for the personnel it was different. The unfolding drama was eagerly followed by all as, at last, a glimmer of light was seen at the end of the tunnel. Perhaps, after all, the end was in sight.

Conversion training continued throughout the summer. Sadly, crashes and deaths were never very far away, yet despite this, the HCU did achieve good results. October 1944 saw 988 hours 50 minutes of day flying and 901 hours 20 minutes of night flying. Though still a part of No 5 Group, it was rumoured that the HCUs were to become part of a new group, No 7, which would contain all the conversion units in Bomber Command.

The repairs to the hard standings being carried out by Sir Robert McAlpine came to an abrupt halt when workmen cut through the mains electric cable, plunging the airfield into darkness for some time. At the same time the much rumoured change to another group became imminent when the AOC sent a

No 1 Pool Flight 1661 HCU RAF Winthorpe in 1944 (via W. Taylor)

signal to the airfields in No 51 Base:

'I send to all ranks in No 52 Base my congratulations on the splendid results which have been achieved over the past eighteen months. I realise the amount of hard work which as fallen on you all. You have made it possible to build up the strength of No 5 Group, which has been able to aim increasingly heavy blows at the enemy. On the eve of your transfer to No 7 Group, I send you my best wishes for the future. I feel confident that we shall be able to earn a similar commendation from our new Group Commander.'

The official change came during November 1944 and, in addition to becoming part of No 7 Group, it was announced that the Stirlings were to be replaced by Lancasters over the coming months. The total strength of the station on 3rd December showed just how cosmopolitan the unit had become. It consisted of 1,580 RAF personnel, 24 RCAF, six RNZAF, one Rhodesian, one South African and one USAAF. The good news regarding the war in general and the fact that new Lancasters would soon be arriving ensured that Christmas day was the best for many years. No flying was possible over this period due to adverse weather, which allowed most of the personnel to spend the first Christmas for several years with their families. Those on duty were served Christmas dinner in the traditional manner before being thanked by Gp Cpt Woodin for their efforts over the past year.

With New Year celebrated it was back to conversion training with the Lancasters, which were arriving daily to replace the Stirlings. Even to the aircraft remaining, tragedy was never far away, as one of the last incidents with the Stirling records. On 14th January 1945, Stirling EH988 was carrying out one of the last training flights with the type. At 11.00 hours, a call was received at Winthorpe saying that a Stirling was seen to crash at Home Farm, Annesley Park, near Mansfield. The caller stated that the starboard engine was on fire and that all around was carnage. The Station Medical Officer and station ambulance proceeded to the scene, where they found that the entire crew had perished. Sqn Ldr S L Cockbain DFC (pilot instructor), Flt Sgt M Barton (navigator), Flt Sgt T Ball (flight eng), Sgt T Littlemore (W/op) and Sgt K Harris (air gunner) could have known very little considering the amount of wreckage that was spread over the

The airmen's mess at RAF Winthorpe. (via W. Taylor)

entire area. Yet again, at 23.30 hours, the SMO and ambulance were called to attend another Stirling crash, this time an aircraft from the neighbouring station of Wigsley. This aircraft flew into high ground whilst descending in low cloud and of the seven crew members, five had been killed, the other two seriously injured. It was a bad beginning to the final year of war.

By February, the last Stirling crew had passed out and No 1661 HCU became once again an all-Lancaster unit. The year also saw the beginning of the end for the Third Reich. On 18th March, the battle of Berlin reached its climax. Since the days of the Polish squadrons flying from Winthorpe to attack the 'Big City', there had been no let-up in the bombing, but 18th March saw the largest bomber force ever assembled. B-24s and B17s (1,251 in all) escorted by 645 Mustang fighters dropped 30,000 tons of bombs on the German capital. Winthorpe and its Polish squadrons had played their part in the early days of this onslaught.

No 1661 HCU now had 32 Lancasters on strength. This

RAF Winthorpe officers' party in 1945, left to right standing: Flt Lt Brunger – Flt Lt W. Clark – Flt Lt H. Rogers - ? – Sqn Ldr J. Grime – Fg Off Paul – Flt Lt Smith. Left to right seated: Sqn Ldr J. Comans – Fg Off Knapp - ? – Flt Lt Macfarlane. (via W. Taylor)

operational standard allowed the trained pilots to move directly to a Lancaster squadron on graduation. The unit now also had the additional task of automatic gun laying training, which involved fighter aircraft flying together with the Lancasters. Winthorpe now became the home for several Hurricanes and Spitfires, types not previously seen at the airfield. It is also fair to say that even at this late stage of the war, the standard of crews passed out remained at a very high level.

The end of hostilities came on 8th May, which the Government declared 'Victory in Europe' day. This was received with great jubilation and a station parade was arranged for 10.00 hours ending with a service of thanksgiving. At last, indeed, the conflict was over and a special VE Day 48-hour pass was issued to all personnel. On 25th May, Sqn Ldr Reynolds from the Air Ministry visited Winthorpe to give lectures on release and re-settlement plans. Despite this finality, however, the unit carried on its work of conversion training accompanied by the usual sad run of crashes and fatalities. On 13th August, Gp Cpt Woodin was posted from Winthorpe and was replaced by Sqn Ldr P O Rose, the reduction in rank indicating that a run-down of the station was imminent. During August this procedure was accelerated, with a final closing down date for No 1661 HCU being set at 10th October along with a change for the station from Bomber Command to Transport Command. The Lancasters were rapidly being dispatched to other units with the final disbandment of the conversion unit coming on 10th September, earlier than planned. Throughout its existence it had played a major part in the training of crews for No 5 Group and later No 7 Group. It had suffered losses and many good men had lost their lives. Now with the war at an end, the need for so many crews was diminishing and No 1661 HCU was to take its place in the history books.

On 20th September 1945, Winthorpe became fully encompassed in Transport Command but in October was reduced to Care and Maintenance, once more becoming just a satellite to Swinderby. It then became a satellite to Syerston in No 4 Group, this base being home to No 1333 Transport Support Training Unit. They operated a selection of aircraft including Halifax, Dakotas, Oxfords and even Horsa gliders. They used Winthorpe as a dropping zone and were joined by No 1331 Heavy Transport Command Unit later in the year. This use continued until Winthorpe was transferred to Maintenance Command with the

The sadly neglected Winthorpe control tower. (via W. Taylor)

arrival of the Central Servicing Development Establishment. This unit carried out documentation of servicing for all current service aircraft, although none were operated by this unit. With its re-location to Swanton Morley in January 1958, Winthorpe became part of Home Command and was to have been used as a hospital by the USAF. This never came about and the station was returned to the Ministry of Defence and placed under Care and Maintenance once again. It continued as such for a few years before being declared inactive in July 1959.

It is fair to say that the entire effort by Bomber Command was a combined campaign of total devotion of the men of the command in the aircraft that they flew. The OTUs and HCUs were an integral part of Bomber Command and Winthorpe played its part well. Today it still remains active, though on a very limited scale. Part of the runway still remains and is used by gliders and light aircraft. The majority of the airfield site is now the Newark and Nottinghamshire showground with the exception of one particular area which houses the very excellent Newark Air Museum. Thus a permanent link with aviation remains and will, hopefully, do so long into the future.

19

WORKSOP

National Grid Reference SK625815, between the A1
and the town of Worksop

We have read in the chapter on airfield construction that several well-known companies were active on building airfields during the expansion programme. Certainly, Wimpey was one of the largest contractors: in 1938, they put in a tender to build thirteen airfields and got the contracts to build seven. The total number of airfields that they eventually built was 93, a considerable number. Around Nottingham, one of the airfields was Worksop (also locally known as Scofton), situated between Worksop and the A1 road.

Although the land was requisitioned in 1942 by the Air Ministry, work on clearing the site did not begin until 1943, when the contractor, George Wimpey, arrived to begin the construction of a standard bomber airfield with three runways, the main runway 2,000 yards long and the others 1,400 yards and 1,100 yards, plus accommodation intended for two squadrons that included two T2 type hangars, 36 dispersed hardstandings and housing for 1,738 RAF and 330 WAAF personnel. The first aircraft to land was a Proctor, on 23 September 1943, when a visiting Air Commodore landed to discuss building progress. Worksop finally opened on 7 November 1943; four days later No 18 OTU moved in from Finningley, where construction of the hard runways was in progress. Worksop was initially designated to supplement Bircotes as a satellite to Finningley as Bircotes had only grass runways, but, in fact, Finningley used both as satellites until the end of 1944.

No 18 OTU was a bomber unit initially formed from the Polish Training Unit and it retained a Polish Flight for most of its existence. Its complement was 54 Wellingtons and four Hurricanes for fighter affiliation, with the Wellingtons used by new bomber crews for multi-engine, navigation, night flying, bombing and gunnery exercises before they moved on to join operational squadrons. Actual types used at Worksop also included Martinets, Oxfords and Tomahawks. Martinets were two seat target tugs of timber construction, while Curtiss Tomahawks were single seat tactical reconnaissance and ground attack fighters designed and constructed in the USA.

As soon as Finningley's runways were complete the HQ moved back there, leaving Worksop as a very busy satellite. In December 1944 the Polish Flight was transferred to No 10 OTU at Abingdon whilst the remainder of the unit transferred here to Worksop to complete its last courses before disbanding on 30 January 1945. However, the runways stayed extremely busy with other units moving in, including No 1 Group (Bomber Command) Communications Flight in March 1945 with a variety of light aircraft; the Night Bomber Technical School arrived from

A Wellington of No 18 OTU that came to grief at Worksop.
(RAF Museum P9817)

Finningley in December 1944 to be reformed as the Bomber Command Bombing School, followed immediately in March 1945 by the RAF Central Vision Training School, which remained until June 1948. The Engine Control Demonstration Unit arrived from Westcott, also in March 1945 with Lancasters, maintaining the type at Worksop until the unit disbanded on 28 September 1945.

The airfield closed in 1948 but was well maintained to be reopened when needed in response to the demand for new aircrews required by the Korean War. After refurbishment the base reopened on 11 August 1952, when No 211 Advanced Flying School formed with three squadrons, No 1 flying Meteor T7 and F8 aircraft whilst Nos 2 and 3 flew the T7 training version. The school flew extremely intensively and utilised the satellite at Wigsley. It was renumbered No 211 Flying Training School, still flying Meteors until disbanding here on 9 June 1958. The school was immediately replaced by No 4 FTS moving in from Middleton St George with a mixture of Meteors and Vampire 3s and T11s, still using Wigsley. The jets were supplemented by No 616 (South Yorkshire) Auxiliary Squadron moving over from Finningley on 23 March 1955 with Meteor F8s, whilst Finningley was closed again for conversion into a V-bomber station. All Auxiliary units were disbanded in March 1957 with 616 being a casualty, but No 4 FTS continued until 9 June 1958, when the school disbanded. Worksop was finally de-requisitioned on 8 December 1960 and many of its buildings were soon demolished as it returned to agriculture. The main runway survives, but little else.

20
THE OTHER AIRFIELDS

Blidworth, Nottinghamshire

National Grid Reference SK590540, SE of Mansfield, near the A614

Lying south east of Mansfield the small grass airfield at Blidworth was established as No 35 Satellite Landing Ground. SLGs were developed by Maintenance Command to provide dispersed storage for Aircraft Storage Units and Maintenance Units. Normally the aircraft were not covered, but sometimes were kept in small blister hangars or even in hides made from tree branches. Usually sited in densely wooded areas, often on estates or in parkland, the SLGs took advantage of the natural camouflage for the parked aircraft, which most often were also camouflaged themselves.

Fifty SLGs were envisaged and 48 opened, with a few being developed into full airfields. Not so Blidworth, which opened in August 1941 as an SLG to No 51 MU at Lichfield with a capacity for 52 fighter aircraft. The single grass runway ran approximately 10/28 (slightly SE to NW) and one end almost touched Blidworth Lodge. It was approximately 800 yards long but appears to have been extended to 1,000 yards – enough to allow Wellington bombers safely to land and take off. Unusually, accommodation was to have been constructed here, with fourteen Nissen huts planned to provide accommodation for approximately 150 men, although it is not recorded whether they were ever actually finished or occupied.

Westland Whirlwind twin-engined fighters are reported to have been stored here but most probably many other, single engined, types were also stored. However, the local ground was marshy and possibly not suitable for storage and No 51 gave up the use of Blidworth in September 1942. However, it continued as a Relief Landing Ground to No 25 (Polish) Elementary Flying Training School's Tiger Moths from Peterborough until the end of 1942, when it appears to have been abandoned; it is probably the airfield with the shortest life span in these counties. What was once the guardroom has been renovated to serve as a bungalow, but otherwise virtually all traces of this small airfield have gone.

Grove Park, Nottinghamshire

National Grid Reference SK734796, east of East Retford

No 38 Satellite Landing Ground opened in August 1942, when an advance party arrived from No 51 MU at Lichfield. It appears that no aircraft were received for storage and by September it was decided to close the landing ground down for the winter. Minimal accommodation was provided, comprising just a few huts for the guards and aircraft handling party. Opened in spring 1943 the runway was serviceable but there is no specific reference to aircraft using the field. On 29 April 1944 the SLG was released by Lichfield and passed to No 27 MU at Shawbury, who used it as a dispersed aircraft storage facility. The types using Grove Park are not recorded and they would have been flown in, concealed and stored until needed. By the end of the war the SLG was no longer required and it was released and closed down on 15 June 1945 with no further use being recorded. The grass runway would have been approximately 1,000 yards long and ran SW/NE.

Hardwick Park, Derbyshire

National Grid Reference SK465645, midway between Chesterfield and Mansfield

Another Satellite Landing Ground, Hardwick Park opened in May 1941 after being constructed by Rendel, Palmer & Tritton with a grass runway of approximately 1,000 yards long running almost N/S, plus 16 acres of storage/parking, which was enough for 65 aircraft. Parented by No 27 MU at Shawbury this mini airfield was located in the grounds of the historic Hardwick Hall, making use of its parkland. The first aircraft to fly in were Boulton Paul Defiants, which arrived on 29 September 1941. However, the ground suffered from water-logging over the winter period, which restricted its (and most other SLGs) use. Other types recorded as stored here include Magister, Dominie and Blenheim.

Many aircraft were stored but the site was spotted by instructors from the Parachute Brigade – particularly the school at Ringway, who started to use the SLG as a dropping zone. The first drop was made on 27 September 1942, when instructors parachuted in from four Whitley aircraft. The HQ of the 1st Parachute Brigade took over use of the Hall itself and the increasing use made it untenable for aircraft storage. The approach was hazardous due to the large trees surrounding the runway so, with effect from 14 September 1943, the RAF gave the SLG up to the Airborne Forces, who stayed until the end of the Second World War when the Hall was returned to its owners and the land de-requisitioned. Now all traces of any military use have disappeared. No doubt the Parachute Brigade used the strip for liaison aircraft but this use is unrecorded.

Orston, Nottinghamshire

National Grid Reference SK780405, 12 miles east of Nottingham

A small grass airfield opened in July 1941 as a satellite to No 16 FTS, which had just moved from Hucknall to Newton. No 16 FTS flew Masters and Oxfords with an establishment of 51 and 33 respectively. This school was very large and specifically trained Polish pilots. Newton could not cope with the huge number of aircraft movements so Orston was pressed into use as a grass airfield with very few facilities but adequate for circuits and bumps and general flying training. Other satellites used simultaneously included Tollerton, Hucknall, Bircotes, Honiley, Ingham, Langar, Sutton Bridge, Syerston and Wellingore. Orston was almost unique, being used by only one unit for its entire life. The use was continuous and heavy until 1st November 1945, when it was closed down. Only one building is known to remain today.

21

THEY CALLED IT 'DAIMLER'

Though this title may seem odd, Daimler was the Luftwaffe code-name for the city of Derby. It was known that the county had become a place of manufacturing and industry since the industrial revolution in the second half of the 18th century. This period had brought the establishment of the Great Midland Railway Works and in the early 1900s the Rolls-Royce company had brought further prosperity to the city. All of this was known to the German Intelligence, making Derby a prime target for Goering's Luftwaffe. Despite this knowledge, only one bomb fell on the aero-engine factory. The city suffered more, but let us concentrate on the industrial plant of Rolls-Royce.

With the factory situated in Nightingale Road, it was not the Luftwaffe that first brought death and destruction to the site. The tragedy began on the morning of 3rd January 1939 when two airmen of No 30 E&RFTS, based at Burnaston airfield, were briefed to carry out a 50 mile cross-country flight to Waddington near Lincoln for the purpose of bringing back another aircraft for the training school. The chief flying instructor, Flt Lt T Reece, and Sgt G A Bell were to fly together in a Miles Magister to collect another Magister training aircraft and ferry it back to Burnaston. Taking off from the airfield at 10.30 am in Magister L8329, the flight to Waddington was uneventful. Landing safely, Flt Lt Reece briefed Sgt Bell about the return flight. The plan was that

The front of the Nightingale Road Works of Rolls-Royce, unaltered from 1940. (Author)

Sgt Bell would follow Flt Lt Reece in the ferry Magister and land back at Burnaston after him. Both aircraft left Waddington together and flew line astern to their home airfield. Arriving over Burnaston, Flt Lt Reece indicated to ground control that he was going to land. Turning finals, he landed at 13.05 pm and taxied to the dispersal area. Switching off his engine, he looked to see if Sgt Bell was in the circuit but saw no-one. Unbeknown to him, as they approached the airfield, Sgt Bell had made a detour from the flight plan that was to cost him his life. He had chosen to deviate from the arranged flight plan and instead carry out his own flying display over the Nightingale Road works. Unfortunately, during a steep turn, the engine on the Magister began to misfire, whereupon the aircraft dived into the ground, causing the death of Sgt Bell. Although an attempt was made to rescue him from the burning wreckage, the heat was too intense, forcing the rescuers back. It was a very sad and unneccesary way to die.

Having mentioned the fact that only one bomb fell on the Rolls-Royce factory, it is interesting to record what raids did take place. The first sightings of enemy aircraft came on Friday 2nd June 1940, when the air-raid sirens wailed indicating that raiders were observed somewhere in the East Midlands. Bombs were, however, dropped only in nearby Yorkshire. For several nights the sirens continued to sound but it was not until the night of 19th/20th August that Derby really received the attention of the Luftwaffe. For much of the night the city was under a yellow or red (attack imminent) air-raid warning. It was a mainly cloudy night but this did not deter a force of He111s penetrating inland with intentions of bombing Derby. As they ranged over the city, bombs were dropped on a foundry, the railway works and indiscriminately on houses. Somehow the enemy missed Rolls-Royce, which was among the main targets. The following night saw enemy aircraft overhead and more bombs were dropped in the area, but again not on the factory.

Wednesday 24th October was a day of brilliant blue sky turning to cloud as evening approached. Manchester was the main target for the He111s of Kampfgeschwader 53 operating out of Lille-Ford in France. One Heinkel, however, found Derby and dropped a single bomb on what the pilot thought was the Rolls-Royce factory. It was not, and again the factory remained

A Luftwaffe He111 over the UK in 1940/41. The He111 was one of the most widely used bombers over this period. (Crown)

unscathed. The rest of the year saw the occasional raider overhead with just sporadic bombs being dropped in the county. The new year, however, saw medium scale attacks renewed on the city.

Wednesday 15th January 1941 saw sunrise at 09.01 hours. Over the UK, the weather was variable, with snow showers and sunshine. Over on the other side of the Channel the cloud was thick enough to give a layer of snow on the ground with further snow showers. This restricted Luftwaffe activity during the daytime with just six enemy aircraft being plotted overland. With clearing skies, the night was to be very different.

At around 18.26 hours, the radar stations along the east coast plotted a large enemy force leaving the Dutch Islands and heading for the UK on a multi-industrial raid. They crossed the coastline between Harwich and Flamborough Head and made a feint of heading towards Birmingham before turning towards the East Midlands. Forty-nine aircraft approached the city but found it covered in thick cloud, giving poor visibility. In fact, the city generated its own protection, for, being industrial, smoke haze was constantly above the buildings. It also had a series of smoke-pots placed in strategic areas, which, when lit, created a smoke-screen thick enough to obscure all but the tallest buildings. With these problems to contend with, the enemy aircraft dropped their bombs through cloud when they estimated they were over the city centre. In fact, they were not and so bombs fell on the Midland railway station and Bliss's factory. In addition, houses in Derby Lane were hit, with further damage in Litchurch Street and the Meadows. Further raids followed during that night with an estimation that between 20.20 and 22.33 hours, at 23.30 hours and between 02.00 and 04.00 hours, 59 tonnes of high explosive bombs were dropped, making it one of the worst nights for Derby. Yet again, Rolls-Royce was not touched.

Many reasons have been put forward as to why the factory escaped serious damage. The industrial haze and smoke-pots that have been mentioned are one. Another theory by historians who have studied the raids on Derby fully is that the Luftwaffe were basing their navigation on outdated Ordance Survey maps which showed incorrect features and locations. The third possibility was the deployment of the Starfish decoy site south of the city at Ticknall. Fires had been lit during this and previous raids in an effort to confuse the enemy. They were also lit on the night of Tuesday 4th/5th February, when Derby, and Rolls-Royce in particular, were the subject of another failed bombing. The Continent was suffering variable cloud, making visibility moderate to poor. Later in the night, fog grounded many German units in France but a unit of Luftflotte 2, KG2 under the command of Oberst Johannes Fink, managed to get airborne and head for the East Midlands. Between 19.45 and 21.55 hours, forty Dornier 17s were over Derby, claiming to have hit the plant. They did drop 28 tonnes of HE bombs and 3,500 incendiaries but the bombing was widely scattered. Turning for home, at least one aircraft came to grief, Do17Z-3 (2907), when it was shot down by Sgt H E Bodien and Sgt E D Jonas flying a Boulton Paul Defiant (with a Merlin engine!) of No 141 Squadron at 21.30 hours. The Dornier crashed at Cowthick Lodge, Weldon, in Northampton killing Oberst H Krisch, Fw H Bahr, Uffz H Kliem and Fw H Vehlemann.

It was target 'Daimler' again over the night of Thursday 8th/9th May 1941. Out of ninety-five aircraft making for Nottingham, the main target on this occasion, twenty-three from Luftflotte 3 proceeded to Derby with Rolls-Royce and another group of industries their main objective. Aiming visually they dropped 14 tonnes of HE bombs and 18,432 incendiaries, causing large fires and damage to the Midland Wagon Works and a TA centre. As described in the chapter on the civilians, this raid planned for Nottingham and Derby went wrong for the Germans, possibly due to the jamming of their navigational beams. It is thought that the beams were centred on Derby but the interference and the small fires that were still burning at Nottingham from the previous evening, fooled them into thinking that this was Derby. The lighting of the Starfish site at Cropwell Butler also was to play a part in the drama. As bad as the raid was on Nottingham, the Starfish certainly prevented the city from receiving a far heavier bomb load. As usual, a German communique incorrectly stated that 'the Rolls-Royce works had been destroyed'.

Nineteen forty-two was the year of the 'Baedeker' raids over the entire country. The enemy, using information taken from *The Handbook for Travellers* written and published by Karl Baedeker in 1839, had drawn up a list of cultural cities in the UK to be attacked. No doubt the cities of Derby and Nottingham were on the list but the raid that took place during the morning of 27th

July 1942 was not a Baedeker raid. What is significant is the fact that it was the only attack to actually hit a building which was part of the Rolls-Royce complex. Air raid warnings went to red at 06.30 hours in Derby. The sirens began their melancholy wailing at the same time as a single Do217E-4 got airborne from its base in Holland. Its only target was Rolls-Royce. Coming in low over Derby and sighting the factory ahead, the pilot, Leutnant Ueberson, gave the order to open the bomb doors. Suddenly the perspex panel in the aircraft nose shattered as the Dornier struck a balloon cable. The cable tantalisingly slid along the leading edge of the wing before the cutter sliced it and it fell away. Four delayed action bombs were dropped before Ueberson managed to pull his aircraft up into cloud cover and turn for home, confident that all the bombs had hit the target. In fact, only one had, the rest fell on houses near the factory, causing twenty-two people to lose their lives and injuring approximately forty. The one bomb which had hit the Steel Store hardly affected production at the plant.

As the years have gone by, much research has been done into just why the enemy, despite their efforts, did not manage to stop

The damage to the steel store at Rolls-Royce incurred by the bomb dropped on 27th July 1942. (Rolls-Royce Heritage Trust)

production at this important aero-engine factory. It is outside the scope of this book to fully investigate the reasons; suffice to say that the bombing of Rolls-Royce is comprehensively covered in a book produced by the Rolls-Royce Heritage Trust (Historical Series No 32) – titled *The Bombing of Rolls-Royce at Derby in Two World Wars*. If the Luftwaffe had succeeded and the 'Daimler' operation had been fully implemented, the Rolls-Royce story may well have been different.

22

ROLLS-ROYCE

I would consider it fair to say that without the Rolls-Royce Merlin aero engine that powered the Hawker Hurricane and Supermarine Spitfire and, to a lesser degree, the Boulton Paul Defiant and the large bombers that followed, the Battle of Britain, and the war in general, may well have been lost for us. That it was not was mainly due to a planned meeting between Henry Royce and the Hon Charles Stewart Rolls on 4th May 1904. From this meeting grew a company which is recognised today as world class in the manufacture of luxury cars and aero engines. Charles Rolls was later to become one of the pioneering aviators in Britain with his greatest achievement being his two-way crossing of the English Channel on 2nd June 1910. Tragically, he was to die one month later when flying his own aeroplane at an air show at Bournemouth, structural failure causing it to crash. He was one of the founders of the Aero Club, later the Royal Aero Club, an establishment that continues today. Despite his death, the company continued to flourish as the affluent members of society clambered to be the first to own and drive luxury cars.

Considering the interest of C S Rolls in aviation, it is strange that the company did not wish to build aero engines prior to the war in 1914, although the first designs were in the process of being drawn up. A year later, however, this changed when the

Rolls-Royce Eagle aero engine was manufactured, the first aircraft to be fitted with these engines being the giant Handley-Page 0/100. The first flight came on Saturday 18 December 1915, when one of these aircraft took off and completed a safe flight. Further engine designs followed, including the Hawk, the Falcon and the Condor, the last being built in August 1918 just before the end of the war. This was the final and largest example of Henry Royce's first generation aero engine.

Between the wars, the company continued to expand its business. At the same time, competition in the aero engine divisions was coming from companies such as Armstrong-Siddeley and Bristol. A disagreement between Air Chief Marshal Trenchard and the board of Rolls-Royce, regarding the introduction of licences for all aero engine production intended for front-line aircraft, nearly ended Rolls-Royce's manufacturing of such engines. With the company refusing to accept the licensing system, at the peak of the problem, Trenchard had demanded 'no more Condors' for the increasing RAF fleet, but luck was to be on the side of Rolls-Royce as the era of experimental aircraft and flying began.

'La Coup'e d'Aviation Maritime Jacques Schneider', better known as the Schneider Trophy competition, had originated in 1912. In the competition seaplanes were flown over a course of at least 150 nautical miles in length. The war saw a cessation of activities but in 1919 Britain became the host nation for a resurgence of the competition. Sponsored by the Royal Aero Club, it was to be held at Bournemouth. Napier Lion engines fitted to the Supermarine Sea Lion were at the forefront, as indeed they were to be for many successive trophy races. Towards the end of 1923, Rolls-Royce began to take an interest in the competition and had in fact produced a 600hp Condor engine giving an estimated speed of 200 mph. However, the aircraft to which it was to be fitted, the Sea Urchin, did not materialise and it was not until 1928 that the company really came on the scene in international competitions.

The previous year had seen the RAF participate fully in the competition. For this, a new unit had been formed called the RAF High Speed Flight, which operated three Supermarine-Napier S.5s. It was this particular year that was to show the world how reliable British built aircraft had become when the two British entries became the only aircraft to finish the race, all the other entries falling by the wayside. Work with the flight continued throughout 1928, although there was no competition that year. In late autumn, Rolls-Royce accepted an Air Ministry invitation to participate in the competition and proposed to put their 825hp 'H' type, or Buzzard, engine into the Supermarine S.6, which had been designed by another aviation pioneer, Reginald Mitchell. He had estimated that the aircraft fitted with this engine would be capable of a speed of around 400 mph with a diving speed of 523 mph and a rate of climb of 5,000 feet per minute. With the date for the competition set for 7 September 1929, Rolls-Royce and Supermarine had set themselves a mammoth task if the aircraft were to be ready in time. Although there were problems throughout this period, two S.6s were ready by the due date and were moved from Calshot to Spithead. Accordingly, a coachload of Rolls-Royce personnel, many of them engineers, travelled to Southampton on the eve of the race. At the last minute problems were found with one of the engines when a piston seized up. Frantic efforts were made to repair the engine overnight and with very little time to spare on testing, the S.6 was slipped into

Reginald Mitchell (left) designer of the Supermarine S6 Schneider Trophy winner, with Henry Royce, who provided its 'R' engine in 1939. (Rolls-Royce plc)

Spithead water. That all the effort and expense had been worth it was amply demonstrated when Flt Lt H R D Waghorn won the contest with an average speed of 328.63 mph. As if to prove a point, four days later, Sqn Ldr A H Orlebar flew the same aircraft (N247) to a new seaplane world record speed of 357.7 mph. Rolls-Royce and the Derby factory had arrived on the competition scene in fine style!

It was to be two years before the competition again took place. By this time an economic squeeze had forced the Government to refrain from subsidising the RAF. A great patriot, Lady Houston, stepped into the breach with an offer of £100,000, which when accepted, incurred a rush for the engineers to get an aircraft ready in time. It was decided by Reginald Mitchell to modify the existing S.6s and incorporate an even more powerful engine, the Rolls-Royce 'R' (for racing), developing 2,350hp. This additional power entailed strengthening modifications to be made and with testing going on day and night, the population of Derby living near the factory began to protest at the amount of noise emanating from the works.

With restraints being placed upon other Governments as well as the British, the 1931 races saw no foreign entries at all. Allowing the event to go ahead on 13 September, the British won unopposed when Flt Lt J W Boothman flew S.6B S1595 at an average speed of 340.08 mph. The world speed record was once again shattered during the afternoon when Flt Lt G H Stainforth attained a world speed record of 379.05 mph in the other S.6B, S1596. The same officer managed to beat this on 29th September when he reached 407.5 mph. This milestone ensured that the trophy would be retained by Britain for ever, as the rules stated that any country winning it three times would win it outright. This achievement pushed forward the designs and developments of future aero engines more quickly than may have been thought possible. No-one at the time knew that eight years on, Britain would be engulfed in a war in which aerial combat would play a major part, even to the extent of winning the war. The Schneider Trophy was part of that long process.

In Germany one year later, the then unknown leader of the National Socialist German Workers Party polled 7 million votes against Hindenburg in the presidential elections of 1932. His name was Adolf Hitler. By 1933 he was Chancellor and with his policy of world domination, he soon seized dictatorial powers.

His promise of returning Germany to its former glory gave hope to the people after their defeat in the First World War and the harsh penalties imposed upon the country by the Versailles Treaty. In 1934 he became Führer and Head of State, a title that saw the beginning of the escalation to a total European war.

It has often been argued that Britain in 1939 was totally unprepared for war. This may well be true for the British Government were still adding up the cost of the first conflict and were reluctant to spend money to rebuild the services. What they did, however, was to select four of the main aero companies to continue their work in design and development of airframes and engines. One of the companies was Rolls-Royce.

One of the more influential engineers within the company at this time was Ernest Hives. He had been with Rolls-Royce from the beginning, joining as a tester in 1908 when the company concentrated on cars. He first became involved in aero engines in 1914 when Royce began work on the Eagle engine. At the age of 30 he became head of the experimental department but returned to the car division with the end of the First World War. By the late 1920s he had once again returned to the aero engines division where he headed development work on the successors to the Eagle engine. Working through a series of uprated engines, all continuing the adoption of bird names, he was to play a prominent part in the engine used for the Schneider Trophy competitions, the Rolls-Royce 'R' engine.

When the company decided to develop a 1,000hp engine, it was Ernest Hives who led the team in developing even further this engine, calling it the PV12, meaning Private Venture 12. It was this engine that was later to evolve as the Merlin. Since the death of Sir Henry Royce in 1933, Ernest Hives had become a hard task master and had set about reorganising almost every aspect of Rolls-Royce. He even arranged for three associates to visit aircraft and engine factories in Germany during 1937. Apparently Hitler was only too pleased to show off the new Germany at this late stage, possibly to ensure that when war came, Britain, seeing the country's military muscle, might decline to go to war and settle for peace. It is recorded that the Rolls-Royce engineers were suitably impressed! Rolls-Royce now had the engine, what was needed was a suitable mount and for this there were two contenders.

By the end of the 1920s it had become obvious to designers that the biplane had reached its limit regarding potential and speed.

Prior to this time T O M Sopwith had become a legend in aviation when his biplanes the Camel, the Pup and others had faced the might of the enemy over the Western Front. His chief test-pilot, Harry G Hawker, started a company during the 1930s and established it in Sopwith's former premises at Kingston-upon-Thames. Sadly, Harry Hawker was killed in a flying accident in 1921 but the company was large enough to continue. In 1924 a new designer, Sydney Camm, came to the company and two years later was given the position of chief designer. At this time Hawker's were still producing biplanes but an Air Ministry specification, F.5/34, called for an aircraft capable of carrying the new Browning machine guns. Both Supermarine and Hawker's submitted designs, the latter following this up by building a one-tenth scale model of the Hawker Interceptor Monoplane and testing it in the wind tunnel of the National Physics Laboratory at Teddington in August 1934.

Test results were encouraging, so much so that on the 4th September, Hawker submitted the design to the Air Ministry. Sydney Camm's design progressed through various stages until on 21 February 1935, enough information on its performance had been gathered to be forwarded to the Air Ministry. The aircraft was expected to have a maximum speed of 330 mph at 15,000 feet, the service ceiling being 32,500 feet with an absolute ceiling of 34,800 feet. These figures convinced the Ministry who offered Hawker's a contract for one high speed monoplane prototype to meet Specification F.36/34. By August 1935 the aircraft was structurally complete and the Merlin engine was lifted into position. On 23rd October, the prototype was taken from the Canbury Park Road works to Brooklands aerodrome, where it was reassembled and made ready for its first flight. Though sporting a silver livery, the RAF roundels and serial number stood proudly out as George Bulman climbed into K5083 on 6th November 1935 and started the Merlin engine. After several taxiing runs he felt sufficiently confident to lift the aircraft off the lush grass of Brooklands. Pulling back on the control column, the Hurricane, as it was now named, took to the air and Britain's first monoplane fighter fitted with a Rolls-Royce engine entered the history books.

In the Supermarine stable, the knowledge gained from developing the Schneider Trophy Seaplanes was applied to a land-based fighter design. With the success of the Schneider racers foremost in his mind, Reginald Mitchell tendered a design to the Air Ministry Specification F.7/30. This again was to be an all metal monoplane with a thick inverted gull wing and short cantilever undercarriage and was to be powered by a Rolls-Royce Goshawk engine. Work went ahead with a prototype being flown by the Supermarine test pilot, J 'Mutt' Summers on 19th February 1934. It proved not to be a success yet Mitchell continued to work on the design; however, with little success for no new prototypes were built. The progress that Hawker's had been making on their monoplane fighter was known to Supermarine and, with the issuing of the Air Ministry Specification F.5/34 on 16th November 1934, Mitchell and his team were authorised by the Board of Supermarine, under the chairmanship of Sir Robert McLean, to proceed with an entirely new fighter design. The suggested power plant was the Rolls-Royce PV12, the same engine that was to power Hawker's design. The new prototype was given the title Company Type No 300 and was covered by Specification F.37/34. On 1st December 1934, Supermarine were given a contract by the Air Ministry for the new fighter and work began on building the Super 300, not yet named the Spitfire, at the Woolston, Southampton factory during 1935. It was at the suggestion of Sir Robert McLean that the official name of the new fighter should begin with the letter 'S'. Several names were banded about, such as 'Shrew', 'Shrike' and even 'Spitfire'. Sir Robert was known to favour the last but, apparently, Reg Mitchell did not and called it 'bloody silly'. However, he did not get the last word and Spitfire it became.

As we have read earlier in the chapter, the prototype Hurricane first flew on 6th November 1935, some months ahead of the Spitfire. By 5th March 1936, however, Spitfire K5054 was ready and 'Mutt' Summers took off to give it its first test flight from Eastleigh near Southampton. It was a successful first flight and Mutt was so impressed by its handling that he told the Supermarine engineers and designers 'not to touch anything'.

Both the Hurricane and the Spitfire were shown to the public for the first time on 27th June 1936 at the Hendon Air Pageant. There then followed many months of testing both aircraft with further modifications being carried out on the Merlin engines. Sadly, on 11th July 1937, Reg Mitchell died of cancer aged 42. It is a shame that he was never to see the culmination of his design become a world beater.

Returning to the Hurricane, the original plan had been to equip all the production aircraft with the Rolls-Royce Merlin I engine. However, in December 1936, ground tests on an up-rated engine were so promising that this Merlin II was selected for both the Hurricane and the Spitfire. With this new power plant, the first production Hurricane flew on 12th October 1937. By the end of the year, seven production Hurricanes were flying and undergoing their manufacturer's clearance tests. Compared with the Spitfire, the Hurricane was relatively easy to produce and so found favour with the Air Ministry. Its canvas-covered fuselage could absorb huge punishment whilst its handling characteristics were superior to the Spitfire's. It fell to No 111 Squadron at Northolt to introduce the new monoplane into operational service when it replaced their ageing Gloster Gauntlets.

A similar pattern was followed by Supermarine when the first production aircraft, K9787, flew at Eastleigh on 14th May 1938. On 27th July it went to A&AEE at Martlesham Heath for handling trials before being allocated to No 19 Squadron at Duxford in Cambridgeshire. No 66 Squadron, the other Duxford squadron, were to receive their first Spitfires on 31st October 1938.

Rolls-Royce, however, was not content to rest on its laurels and alongside the Merlin were developing the Griffon and the

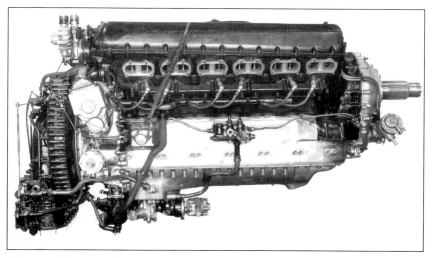

The magnificent Rolls-Royce Merlin III engine. (Rolls-Royce plc)

Vulture engines. At Derby, the production of the Merlin III engine was given top priority. The Rolls-Royce factories at Crewe and Glasgow played their part in ensuring that production was kept to a peak as the number of Hurricanes and Spitfires produced increased. Over this same period, many of the non-production staff, ie drawing, technical and designs people, were moved from the main Derby works to the nearby village of Belper. The reason given was that, should an enemy raid occur on the main works, not only were there insufficient shelters for the increased number of employees, but it would be disastrous if the technical people should perish in a raid.

At the beginning of 1939, Derby was expected to produce 3,200 engines a year, which were almost entirely Merlins. At this stage they were mainly intended for the Hurricanes and Spitfires of Fighter Command but other aircraft such as the single-engined Fairey Battle light bomber and the turreted fighter, the Boulton Paul Defiant, were also fitted with the Merlin. In order to cope with this demand, Derby was further extended and the shadow factories were forced to take on more labour, not an easy task when most able-bodied men were in the forces. When difficulty

Production of the Merlin engines continues, uninterrupted by enemy bombs. (Rolls-Royce Heritage Trust)

arose, women were recruited and trained in various roles. Long and frustrating delays in production were apparent as unskilled labour was brought up to the standards required to do the job. Gradually output did improve, as by June 1941 the target of 200 engines per month was attained and by March 1943, output exceeded 400 per month.

The company had looked at the possibility of having Merlins made in the USA as early as 1938. Several companies had been considered including Pratt and Whitney and Packard. Ernest Hives already knew of the enormity of the task, which he pointed out to Lord Beaverbrook, the Minister of Aircraft Production, in a letter dated 8th July 1940. In it he mentions the possibility of sending Rolls-Royce engineers to the USA in order to assist in the production of Merlin engines. He further emphasised that just because the USA had been sent Merlin drawings, this did not mean that they were in a position to manufacture.

In fact, Packard very nearly did not get the contract, for in June 1940, the question of producing the engine abroad was taken out of the hands of Rolls-Royce and placed in that of Lord Beaverbrook and the Air Ministry. Somehow the *New York Herald Tribune* got hold of a story relating that Lord Beaverbrook had given the Ford Motor Company a contract to produce 6,000 engines. Amidst a flurry of correspondence and cables between Derby, Packard and Ford, and, whilst the story was later proved to be true, the matter was settled when Ford declined; the intricacy of the aero engine would not have suited Ford's production methods. Once this was known, the Packard Company was offered the contract and accepted it. The first order was for 9,000 engines of which 6,000 were for the British Government and 3,000 for the American. In later years, Fords of Dagenham were to become one of the shadow factories producing the engines, but this was at Trafford Park, Manchester and Derby was not very far away. However, the production of the Merlin in the USA was a great success. From the signing of the contract on 3rd September 1940 up to the production of the first engine in September 1941, a great achievement was made. By the time production ceased, 55,000 engines had been produced by the Packard plant in Detroit. Much of its development data lies in the archives of Packard but, suffice to say, if Rolls-Royce and the Government had not allowed this contract to go ahead, the present day may well have been very different.

Back in the UK, the Merlin was progressing through various stages of development. By the time the Battle of Britain began in July 1940, most of the RAF's Hurricanes and Spitfires were powered by Merlin IIIs. By autumn a number of the later Spitfires were fitted with the Merlin XII, giving them additional altitude performance. Later versions of the Hurricane, mainly the Hurricane II, were powered by the Merlin XX, which had an improved supercharger design with a two speed supercharger drive.

Of the supercharger it must be said that the increased power of the Merlin would never have come about without it. With the principle being invented in 1906, it was an expert in the 1920s, one Jimmy Ellor, who further developed the idea. Further work was carried out by Dr Stanley G Hooker, who eventually became supervisor of supercharger development. Whilst the basic operation of the unit was in itself relatively simple, calculating the equations was the difficult part. The power of an engine depends on the mass of fuel and air it can consume in a given time. The job of a supercharger is to provide more of both. In order that the reader may appreciate the gigantic strides taken by Rolls-Royce in up-dating the Merlin, consider that in 1936 the power of the engine was 1,000bhp, but this had grown to over 2,000bhp by 1944. This increase in power also nearly doubled the altitude at which the engine would operate most efficiently – from 16,000 feet to 30,000 feet.

It was not, however, just the Merlin engine that was to give the RAF the upper hand, for running alongside the design and development of the Merlin was the Griffon. The first run of a Griffon engine, serial No 1, was on 6th January 1933, but at this early stage the programme got no further as priority was given to the Merlin. Not until 1939, and at the instigation of Ernest Hives, was a new Griffon programme introduced. The first engine was run on 30 November 1939, and by progressing through a series of modifications and up-dates, by December 1940 it was classified as the Griffon IIB. This version performed well from the start and with a two stage, two speed supercharger fitted, the power increased from 1,700hp to 2,300hp and a rated altitude from 14,500 feet to 26,000 feet.

By late 1939, interest in the Griffon had reached the Air Ministry and Supermarine and it was decided to fit one into a Spitfire. With more pressing events to attend to, the first flight of

The handsome stained glass window located in the main hall of the Derby works of Rolls-Royce plc.(Rolls-Royce plc)

a Griffon-engined Spitfire did not take place until 27th November 1941. With a MkIV Spitfire in the capable hands of test pilot Jeffrey Quill carrying out the first test flight, the combination proved such a success that, in the words of the pilot: 'It became one of our favourite aeroplanes.' Once again, Rolls-Royce had a winner. Plans went ahead to fit a Spitfire with a big two-stage Griffon engine. When completed, Jeffrey Quill tested the aircraft against a German FW190 and a British Typhoon. With the display taking place before a selection of VIPs at Farnborough, the Spitfire outpaced both aircraft and, again in the pilot's words: 'The sensation was considerable.' The Griffon remained in service throughout the war and into peacetime, the last aircraft to be fitted with it being the big four-engined Avro Shackleton, which had contra-rotating Griffon-powered propellers and remained in service until 1991.

By the end of 1944, Spitfires and Mosquitos were carrying the war back to Germany whilst the Lancaster bomber roamed over the major German cities, causing destruction and devastation. With the Merlin and the Griffon now approaching their maximum stages of development, the words 'gas turbine' were becoming very prevalent.

It is not within the realms of this book to include an in-depth history of the jet engine but it is part of the Rolls-Royce story and must be included. Two people were mainly responsible for its invention: Dr A A Griffiths of the Royal Aircraft Establishment's Engines Experimental Department and an RAF officer, Frank Whittle. It was the latter who envisaged aircraft flying at speeds of 500 mph at heights where the air was rarer. Though initially not sure of the propulsion method, in October 1929 Whittle realised that the exhaust from the jet nozzle would propel the aircraft. Discussing his invention with two RAF colleagues, it was suggested that he approach the Air Ministry for financial backing. This he duly did but shortly after received a letter from them stating that the engine was impractical due to the fact that the materials needed to withstand high stress and high temperature did not exist at this time. Though saddened by their response, Whittle took out a patent on his engine in January 1930. However, over the intervening years, he allowed his patent to lapse saying that he had 'lost hope of the successful development of the turbo-jet engine'.

Fate now played a hand and, encouraged by the two former

Sir Frank Whittle, inventor of the Jet Engine. (Archive)

Cranwell colleagues who were prepared to put up the money for further research, Whittle formed a company, naming it 'Power Jets Ltd'. Development work continued throughout 1938 and 1939, with the Air Ministry, encouraged by what they now saw, coming onto the side of Whittle's company and offering to pay for spares and modifications. A further visit by the Air Ministry in January 1940 brought even further support for Power Jets but it soon became obvious that, whilst the company could carry out experimental work, it could not undertake wholesale production of the engine. It was Whittle who suggested that the Rover Company should be brought in to take up this task. At around the same time, the Gloster Aircraft Company were asked to design an aircraft capable of carrying the new engine.

Design and development continued but the limited experience of the Rover Company led to difficulties and long delays in production of the engine. It had been suggested that the prototype production engine should be ready for installing in an

Frank Whittle's first engine, which was installed in the E.28/39 for its first flight on 15th May 1941. (Archive)

aircraft by early 1942, but with Rover's problems this rapidly became impossible. Another problem had emerged when co-operation between Power Jets and Rover was not what it should have been. It was found that for some time Rover had been carrying out their own development work when they should have been concerned with the production side. Ironically, it was at this stage that Rolls-Royce entered the frame. In May 1941, the Air Ministry suggested to Ernest Hives that Derby might be able to give some assistance to Rover by manufacturing certain parts of the engine that caused difficulty. Hives agreed but emphasised that he would like Rolls-Royce to play a larger part than just making 'bits and pieces!' The company had been well aware of developments with the jet engine and had, in fact, already recruited A A Griffiths, the first pioneer in this field, to continue his development work. The collaboration with Whittle soon produced results as Rolls-Royce began making many components for both companies.

Gloster meanwhile had been busy developing an aircraft to carry the new engine and by April 1941 the Gloster/Whittle E.28/39 was ready for flight. On 8th April, Gerry Sayer, the Gloster test pilot, not only taxied the aircraft but actually took off and flew for two or three yards from Gloster's airfield at Brockworth. His comments: 'The engine is very smooth, indeed no vibration was observed in the pilot's cockpit. The engine ran very well throughout the taxiing trials.'

It was at Cranwell, a place that Whittle knew so well, that the first proper flight took place. As news of the successful flight reached the Secretary of State for Air, Sir Archibald Sinclair, and the Air Ministry, the pendulum swung full circle and the Ministry now offered Whittle any help that he required. A target was set at 1,200 engines and 500 aircraft, the first to be available in June 1942. This, however, was a little optimistic for Whittle knew there were still many technical problems to be solved.

Problems of another sort were still apparent between Power Jets and Rover, so much so that the Ministry of Aircraft Production suggested that Rover hand over its development and production sections to Rolls-Royce. The Ministry further suggested that Rolls-Royce take over Power Jets but this was not to be. However, with Rover out of the running, Power Jets became strongly in favour of Rolls-Royce alone manufacturing the engine. With these problems settled came a new urgency for

GLOSTER E.28/39

Powered by: One 860 lb (390 kg) st
Power Jets (Whittle) W.1 centrifugal-flow
turbojet engine
Wing span: 29 ft 0 in (8.84 m)
Length: 25 ft 3¾ in (7.72 m)
Wing area: 146.5 sq ft (13.6 m²)
Gross weight: 3,700 lb (1,678 kg)
Max speed: 338 mph (544 km/h) at
15,000 ft (4,570 m)
Accommodation: Crew of 1

First flight: 15 May 1941
The data above apply to the first E.28/39
prototype with original engine. Later, with
a 1,700 lb (770 kg) st Power Jets
W.2/500 engine, it flew at approx 450
mph (724 km/h). The second prototype,
fitted with a Rover W.2B engine of 1,200
lb (544 kg) st, reached a speed of 466 mph
(750 km/h) during tests.

A   SECRET

GLOSTER AIRCRAFT CO. LTD.

TEST FLIGHT REPORT No.: 1

PILOT P.E.G.Sayer.

Type of Test :   1st Flight. General experience of the type.

Date and Time of Start 15.5.41.   1940 hrs.   Duration 17 mins.

AIRCRAFT : Type and No.   E.28/39. W.4041.

Type of Undercarriage Dowty nose wheel type. All retractable.

Other Features Main wheel lever suspension type. Nose wheel strut type.

AIRSCREW : Type and No.   No airscrew fitted with this method of propulsion.

Dia. :

Pitch Setting Fine   Coarse

Ground Clearance Flying Position   Tail on Ground

ENGINE : Type and No. Whittle Supercharger Type W.1.

Reduction Gear

R.P.M. O.G. Fine Pitch 16500 Take-off.   Coarse Pitch

Boost O.G.

Type of Air Intake

Radiator Stbd radiator blanked off. Port radiator in circuit.

Other Features

WEIGHTS
CARRIED : Fuel Paraffin 50 galls.   Oil 1 gall.

Cooling Liquid 3.5 galls water.

Total Weight 3441 lb. estimated from Two C.G.

C.G. Position .284 A.M.C. U/C Down. .297 A.M.C. U/C Up calculated from
(Tare C.G.

Loading Sht. No. 142   Date 7.5.41.

REMARKS :

Exhaust System   Nose wheel leg total travel 12" as against 10" on
Cooling System   original nose wheel leg fitted for taxying trials at
Oil System   Brockworth. Static travel 6" instead of 7" on the first leg.
Guns and Mountings Nose wheel strut pressure reduced from 140 lbsq.in. to
Bombs and Racks   115 lbsq.in. Tyre pressure reduced from 35 lbsq.in. to
Sights   30 lbsq.in.
Nav. and Ident. Lamps Steering on nose wheel 11° either side of the centre line
Aerial   Brakes on all three wheels.
Fairing

Type of Cockpit Heating

Pitot Position & Type

TEST INSTRUMENTS :

Icsn. Altimeter No. :   Calibrated

A.S.I. Instrument No. :   "

R.P.M.   "   "   "

Boost Gauge   "   "   "

Air Temp.   "   "   "

                                                        139

Signature of Pilot   [signature]

The official Gloster report on the first flight of the
Gloster E.28/39. (Gloster Aircraft Co. Ltd)

the engines, now known as W.2B. Within days, nearly 2,000 men and women were put to work on getting the engine ready for RAF service. By May 1944, the first Gloster Meteor Is were delivered to the RAF powered by Whittle's design, which Rolls-Royce had named the Welland. After a test period at the Royal Aircraft Establishment at Farnborough, the Meteor entered operational service with No 616 (South Yorkshire) Squadron of the Royal Auxiliary Air Force. Flying from Manston in Kent, they became heavily involved in the VI campaign. The gas turbine powered aircraft, however, saw limited use in the Second World War. It was the peacetime air force that saw the rapid expansion in this form of aero engine. Yet again, Rolls-Royce rose to the forefront of this technology and today it is four Rolls-Royce (Bristol)/SNECMA Olympus 593 re-heated turbojets that power the Aerospatiale/BAE Concorde and the RB-211 that powers many Boeing 747 and 777 airliners.

Rolls-Royce has become world famous for the quality of its products, and it was from the historic meeting of Henry Royce and the Hon C S Rolls on 4th May 1904 at the Midland Hotel in Manchester that it has grown to be a company that personifies the 'best of British'. Long may it remain so.

A Gloster Meteor T7 powered by a Rolls-Royce Welland engine, a design based on Whittle's jet engine. (MAP)

23

CIVILIANS AT WAR

'We have been forced at last to go to war. We tried again and again to prevent this war and for the sake of peace we put up with a lot of things happening which ought not to have happened. But now we are at war and we are going to make war and persevere in making war until the other side has had enough of it. We are going to persevere as far as we can, to the best of our ability, which is not small and always growing.'

So spoke Winston Churchill, then First Lord of the Admiralty, in 1939. Certainly, regarding the civilian population, persever-ance was the word. In literal terms it means 'not to give in', something that the people of Nottinghamshire and Derbyshire never did.

With the invasion of Czechoslovakia by Germany in March 1939, most of the civilian population knew that war was inevitable. As if in preparation for the hardship and shortage of food that every housewife knew would come, the Women's Land Army was formed in June of the same year. The slogan 'Lend a hand on the Land' appeared everywhere and thousands of volunteers came forward to replace some of the labour that the farmers had lost in the call-up. With the help of the Land Army, food production was dramatically stepped up in an attempt to make the country self sufficient, as importing food by sea was difficult and dangerous. The scheme was administered by women with the aim of attracting girls from factories, shops and offices who had always wanted a job in the open air.

Because they were engaged in essential war work, the members of the Women's Land Army were kitted out in a distinctive, practical brown uniform. The state did not provide everything and the girls had to surrender some of their clothing coupons in exchange for the uniform. They also had to supply their own underwear and nightwear. The wide brimmed hat worn by the girls became a trademark and it could be adapted to any shape that best suited its wearer. Once the women were kitted out, a limited training programme was forthcoming as many of them had not worked on farms. Unlike the regular armed services, the Women's Land Army had no opportunities for promotion. However, to keep up their morale during the long hours and bad weather, Land Army honorary director, Lady Denman, sent letters to all the girls every six months congratulating them on their sterling work. Derby was to receive additional felicitations from the county chairwoman, the Duchess of Devonshire, as the local magazine *The Derby Ram* recorded over Christmas 1941. 'At a Xmas party held to celebrate

A company of Land Army girls listening to Lord Woolton, Minister of Food, during 1941. (SE Newspapers)

1941, some 51 girls attended. It was a bevy of healthy, happy Rosalinds whose appearance proclaimed the wholesomeness of their occupation.' Congratulating them, the Duchess said that she was proud of the Land Army and stated that there was no work more important than theirs, for people could not work if they did not have food to eat. What the girls had done was a credit to them and they could be looked upon as the backbone of the country. There followed a rousing chorus of the Women's Land Army Song, which I am privileged to print within these pages.

'Backs to the land, we must all lend a hand,
To the farms and fields we go,
There's a lot to be done though we can't fire a gun,
We can still do our bit with the hoe.'

Without these girls, food during the war may have proved an even bigger problem.

With the invasion of Poland, the war came very much closer and the evacuation of mothers and children, sometimes together, sometimes separately, from the cities began. The operation was

Many London children and families were evacuated to Nottingham and Derby. Around one and a half million families left London. (Archive)

code-named 'Pied Piper' and the child evacuees were organised into school groups with labels attached to their lapels or belts indicating their name, school and religion. With gas mask holders hanging from their shoulders and small cases or carrier bags containing clothes and some food, many a tearful little boy or girl clung to their mothers until the very last moment of parting. The majority travelled by train from the big cities to the comparative safety of the countryside.

The facts and figures for the September 1939 evacuations make astonishing reading. On the move were 827,000 school children, 524,000 pre-school children and their mothers, 12,000 pregnant mothers and 103,000 teachers and helpers. From Derby alone, 1,000 evacuees were sent to the Chesterfield/Clay Cross area, 1,000 to North Wingfield, 300 to New Tupton and Pilsley, 250 to Stonebrook, 200 to Shirland and 150 to Morton. Once the parting with parents was over, the children settled down on the train journey only to be frightened when they arrived at their destination and met their new 'parents'. They often arrived homesick, dirty and hungry, which slowed the allocation of children to homes as some families would only take children that looked clean and tidy. Once settled, though, the majority of children from the cities revelled in the luxury of the countryside and all its attractions. However, the first wave of evacuation did not last long as the period known as the 'phoney war' continued for a while and many had returned home by Christmas. Once war finally came the process of evacuation started all over again and carried on throughout the war, with the final phase being in the summer of 1944. The Government planned to move about 3.5 million people. The final total was far less – around 1.5 million.

When war became imminent, the wireless, as the radio was known in those days, became the voice of the civilian population. It gave out notices of importance regarding their protection, as well as a mixture of news, comedy and music. It gave advice, such as that given by the Radio Doctor in attempting to keep us all well. I quote: 'And how's your tummy feeling this morning? Is it a little heavy, a trifle windy? What you need is a stable diet and today I am going to tell you just what that should consist of in these troubled times.' The radio also informed you of where your nearest shelter was or where the nearest Civil Defence post was. And, of course, it was used for propaganda. Even the German propaganda machine found its way onto the British wireless, one of the most famous figures being 'Lord Haw Haw'. William Joyce was an American-born supporter of the Nazi cause, whose opening signature was 'Jairmany Calling'. He had lived in London before moving to Berlin to begin broadcasting his nauseating, misleading information to the British public. With his 'upper crust' accent, he fooled vast numbers of people into actually believing what he said. With the end of the war, William Joyce was tried for treason and hanged.

The wireless was also the medium for announcing the formation of an organisation called the Local Defence Volunteers. It was on 14th May 1940 that Sir Anthony Eden, then Secretary of State for War, broadcast the appeal:

"Since the war began, the Government have received countless enquiries from all over the kingdom for men of all ages who are, for one reason or another, not at present engaged in military service, and who wish to do something in the defence of their country. Well, now is your opportunity. We want large numbers of such men in Great Britain who are British subjects between the ages of 17 and 65 to come forward now and offer their service in order to make assurances doubly sure. The name of the new force

A civil defence exercise involving children takes place during 1939 in Nottingham. (Archive)

which is now to be raised will be the Local Defence Volunteers."

Within twelve hours of this broadcast over one hundred men had enrolled in Nottingham's Guildhall. The LDV became the butt of many jokes including the fact that the initials might stand for 'Look, duck and vanish'. In fact, on 23rd July, the LDV was discarded, to be replaced by the Home Guard. Initially the force was ill-equipped to repel any invasion. Armed with pick-axe handles, hay forks and any other hard, large object, they would go out night after night on patrol keeping an eye out for enemy parachutists. This was obviously not acceptable and the issue of real guns came later, including the use of farmers' sporting and shot guns. The uniform was just an armband displaying the initials LDV, but towards the end of 1940 the issue of a standard army battle-dress became the norm.

Several factories in both counties organised their own platoons of the Home Guard and, in the case of Nottingham, a platoon called The Trent River Patrol was formed a month after the LDV. In June 1940 a headquarters was set up in a cafe at Gunthorpe with Lt Cdr Ford as its commanding officer. Armed with real rifles, the patrol started its nightly vigil. Its duties were to repel any enemy craft found on the river, to maintain lines of communications, to ensure the free passage of boats through the area and to ferry troops to strategic points should an invasion ever occur. The latter, of course, thankfully never did happen but it may have given the enemy a shock had he attempted to do so upon seeing the Blue Ensign and a Blue and White Pennant fluttering in the wind.

Derby was to see many of the industries form their own battalions. Derby Cable Works became one of the first, followed by British Celanese. At a parade and inspection for the former unit by Brigadier-General E C W D Salthall, the county commandant, held in August 1940, some of the men had to parade in civilian clothes. At this time only a few had the Home Guard uniform but what they lacked in suitable clothing was made up by the fact that they had received the first rifles. It was noted at the time that one Lancashire regiment was armed only with six spears! By March 1942, four squads of the Women's Home Defence Force had been formed in the counties, where recruits were given instruction on firing a rifle, grenade throwing, and even how to handle a Smith anti-tank gun. That they were brave is in no doubt as the following excerpt from an ARP diary for

Preparing for invasion. The road signs come down in Derby.
(Derby Evening News)

The Trent River Patrol in action. Part of the Home Guard, it became known as 'Dad's Navy'. (Archive)

Nottingham states: 'With the central control telephone boards operated entirely by women, a particularly heavy bomb fell in the vicinity of the headquarters. The whole place rocked, the lights went out but the emergency lighting set was immediately brought into use. Dust filled the air choking the girls and although some were becoming tearful, the command 'sit still' from the chief restored their confidence. They sat there hour after hour plugging in and taking or sending essential messages.'

Just how keen the civilians were to join the Home Guard is indicated by the fact that by 27th May 1940, 3,900 men in the city of Nottingham and 9,048 men in the shires had volunteered. The Home Guard was a bargain to the country, the cheapest army of its kind that any country possessed. They suffered fewer casualties than any comparable army, although 1,206 Home Guard were killed on duty or died of wounds, the majority during the Flying Bomb period. Another 557 were injured, mainly from handling explosives for which they were not adequately trained. Had the enemy invaded, there is no doubt that the Home Guard, both men and women, would have fought as valiantly as those on service overseas.

Perhaps the most vital roles in wartime broadcasting were those of informing the populace of how the war was going and

*Lewis Gun instruction complete with gas masks in Highfields Park,
Nottingham University. Notts Home Guard. (Archive)*

helping everyone through everyday life – from advice on making
the most of the rations to the easy way to erect your air-raid
shelter. With the expected blitz upon the mainland, public
shelters were planned and built in all the major cities. In
Nottingham, surveys were undertaken to estimate how many
existing cellars and vaults could offer any sort of protection. With
the city being built upon an underground system of caves, some
were used as shelters. In other cases, brick shelters were built
around shopping areas and protected on the outside by
sandbags. Nottingham City Council certainly had foresight for
by 1939, before the war started, there were 187 public shelters
ready for use. These would have accommodated 24,000 people
but work was already in hand for protecting a further 5,000. By
1941, the city had 288 public shelters plus many more that were
built for the protection of employees in factories, schools,
hospitals and so on.

The most common shelter for families, however, was the
Anderson Shelter. Named after the designer, Dr David A
Anderson and not, as is so often thought, Sir John Anderson, the

Nottingham's Home Guard during an exercise in March 1943. They are driving a Bren Gun carrier. (Archive)

Secretary of State for Home Affairs at the time, it became a familiar sight in many gardens. It could be erected on the surface or semi-sunk into the ground with the added outside protection of sandbags. Cheap to produce, it consisted of corrugated steel sheets bolted together and placed over a curved frame, which was in turn bolted to the sheets. Rather small in size, the shelter could accommodate a maximum of six people sitting; they were not designed for sleeping. They were also prone to flooding during heavy rain and, without any form of heating, were very cold in autumn and winter.

In Nottingham, the worst instance of flooding was on the Elloughton Estate off Western Boulevard. The problem became so bad that the city engineer wrote to the Home Office requesting brick shelters instead of Andersons. Suffice to say, he did not get them! Initially the shelters were supplied in large numbers free of charge. Government policy, however, changed in 1939 when it was stated that people whose earnings were over a certain amount should pay, at prices ranging from £6 14s to £10 18s (£6.40 to £10.90). Nottingham supplied 23,650 Anderson shelters; Derby considerably fewer.

The other main 'personal' shelter was the Morrison. Named after the Minister for Home Security, Herbert Morrison, this was

Repairs to houses in the Hood Street area of Nottingham in August 1940.
Note the Anderson Shelter. (Notts Archives)

an indoor shelter which took the form of a large, square, thick metal top, which could be used as a table, supported on four metal posts. The sides were covered in wire mesh and it could comfortably sleep four children or two adults. So strong was it that it offered very good protection if a house was bombed.

The final shelter was the Surface Shelter. Brick built, they were usually sited in areas of dense population such as flats or row upon row of terraced houses. Prone to overcrowding during air-raids, they could be stuffy and smelly with sanitation proving a problem, especially during long periods of occupation.

On 9th July 1939 came a trial of the blackout. This was mainly for householders, who were asked to cover all their windows at night in any type of black material they could find. There was an instant rush to the shops to buy blinds, black sacking, black paint and even cardboard. The windows on buses and trains were all blacked out with just a small slit to allow people to see where they were. Local ARP wardens were then tasked with inspecting all areas to see whether any chink of light could be seen. By the end of the month, council workers in Nottingham and Derby and the surrounding towns and villages were out in force painting white bands around all upright obstacles lest, with no street lighting, people should walk into them. Kerbs and traffic islands were given the same treatment and all traffic lights were fitted with black-out cowls. Vehicle headlights were fitted with hoods, allowing just a slit of light to be seen. It was said that when these restrictions were first introduced, the accident rate in both counties increased dramatically. Later, as people became more aware, it dropped to a normal level. The total blackout caused many problems and from October 1939 certain modifications were introduced to reduce the hazards. The public were allowed to carry hand torches provided they were muffled with toilet paper. By Christmas of the same year, churches were allowed to partially light up for the many services associated with the period. Bad road junctions were allowed 'glimmer' lighting. It fell to the ARP Wardens to see that these restrictions were carried out effectively and it was their cry of 'Put that b **** light out' that became the butt of many comedians' jokes.

Civil defence became all important during the opening phases of the war. In 1939 there were 1,500,000 defence personnel, consisting mostly of volunteers. With the outbreak of war, the civil defence system integrated with local government and included control of the ambulance, fire and police services. The Civil Defence Warden was to be the eyes and ears of the organisation. Dressed usually in a blue boiler suit complete with a tin hat, it was his duty to see that in the event of an air-raid, the public in the street were ushered into one of the sand-bagged brick shelters that were clearly marked. It was also his duty to write up the 'war log' that every city, town and village kept, recording any incident regarding the war. The chain of command for the Civil Defence organisation ran from the regional headquarters through the group headquarters to the borough. This headquarters was usually a town hall or government building which was responsible for integrating the civil defence system with local government. Next to the borough lay the district, which in turn led to the Civil Defence posts and ARP posts. That it worked was proved in the early days of the war, and as that progressed so did the efficiency of the operation.

The men of the Auxiliary Fire Service, so ably recruited during 1938, were intended to increase the regular fire brigade numbers.

The auxiliaries fought alongside the regulars with ever increasing strength. When war became imminent, all AFS and regular fire service units were issued with steel helmets and respirators. The pay rates were rather frugal considering the dangers of the job, with AFS full-time crews being paid £3 and £2 for women, youths aged 17–18 years £1 5s (£1.25) and even younger earning just £1. Although later incorporated into the National Fire Service on 22nd May 1941, they were justly proud of their past auxiliary status. With this amalgamation, the National Fire Service was divided into twelve regions, each being sub-divided into fire forces. Derby became encompassed within Fire Force No 7 whilst Nottingham was in Fire Force No 8.

It was probably the rationing that hit the counties' housewives the most. For them the daily struggle with ration cards, huge queues and shortages made life very difficult. Rationing was first introduced in January 1940 and it was butter, sugar, bacon and ham that were the first to go. Offal, fish and that basic diet, potatoes, were left untouched and it was these items that came to comprise the national diet. It became a crime to throw any food away, especially bread, which even when mouldy could be

A depot of Nottingham's National Fire Service hold an exercise. (Archive)

turned into bread pudding or similar. Plans had been made by the Government to introduce what was called the 'Basal Diet' for every person. This would consist of a daily ration of 12oz of bread, 1lb of potatoes, 2oz of oatmeal, 1oz of fat, 6oz of vegetables and six-tenths of a pint of milk. The idea was never implemented and by August 1942, an adult ration had settled down to 1lb of meat a week, 4oz of ham and bacon, 8oz of sugar, 8oz of fat and 8oz of cheese.

People were encouraged to 'Dig for Victory', which often meant them digging up lawns and any spare unoccupied area of ground in which to grow their own vegetables. For children it seemed a dream come true when soap became very scarce and was put on ration. In hope, they thought 'no soap – no washing'. Mothers, however, had other ideas and would use any type of cleaning fluid they could find. It was not, however, all bad. One of the nicer touches came in November 1941 when the Ministry of Food made a decision to double the allocation of dried fruits in order that housewives could make a Christmas cake. The ration was increased from 6oz to 12oz.

Although times were hard, housewives kept a sense of enterprise and good humour nearly always prevailed. The joke 'if you see a queue, join it' was to come full circle for it was not uncommon for housewives to join one even if they did not know what was at the other end. The sight of long queues forced Sir Stafford Cripps to tell the House of Commons in February 1942 that 'personal extravagance must be eliminated altogether'. Help came from America between the summers of 1940 and 1941 with the arrival of the first Lend-lease goods. These provided the housewife with versatile canned meats such as Spam, canned fruit and other goods. Despite all, every woman was determined to make her contribution of 'making do' to see that the country was not starved into submission.

Housewives again came to the rescue when an appeal by Lord Beaverbrook, Minister of Aircraft Production, requested that they allow any utensils such as aluminium kitchenware to be put to the war effort. The women of Derby and Nottingham responded instantly and pots and pans, kettles, shoe-trees, coffee-pots, metal railings and every sort of aluminium article was placed in bags and sent down to the Westminster headquarters of the Women's Voluntary Service. This collection was later extended to bathroom fittings, coat hangers, vacuum cleaners, cigarette cases and all things metal. Once melted down, the metal was used for aeroplanes to help Britain's drive for air supremacy and once again, the housewife was only too pleased to help.

Many women, not content with just struggling to feed their family, wanted to 'do their bit' in industry too. At the LNER depot in Derby, women were employed in making concrete sleepers. Firms like Qualcast, Ley's Malleable Castings and E W Bliss gave up production of some of their usual commodities in order to make millions of grenade, shell and bomb casings. Between September 1940 and the end of 1941, the munition industries needed to recruit, due to many of their male employees joining the armed forces. Many women in the 19–24 age group volunteered for heavy engineering work and although their pay was roughly half that of their male counterpart, they put their backs into the jobs. Women were also employed on essential services such as buses and trains, carrying out a variety of work. Train guards, porters, ticket collectors on both buses and trains, signalwomen, boiler cleaners – nothing was to prove too hard for the wartime women.

So far we have generalised on what every civilian in the country had to do to make ready for war. Concentrating on the two counties shows that in addition to hardship in the home, the enemy bombers brought tragedy to many families. In preparation for what was to come, 16th October 1939 saw the Nottingham Comforts Fund start. This was a gesture by the people of Nottinghamshire to see that twice a year the cash equivalent of 50 cigarettes was cabled to every man serving in a Nottingham unit. By 1944, with 2,550 Nottinghamshire men in POW camps, the fund was additionally sending 200 cigarettes every six weeks.

The first day of January 1940 saw the launch of the Nottingham War Savings Campaign, intended to raise money to help the war effort. Not far behind was Derby who, on Thursday 7th August 1941, celebrated a campaign called 'Speed the Tank', when two tanks named 'Matilda' and 'Valentine' paid a visit to the market place. During the previous 18 months, Derby had raised over £5,000,000, but more was needed. Lt E Cook, the tank commander, thanked the Mayor and people, saying, 'We are all waiting to get at the huns and with these tanks, I think the day will come when we can fix them.' In line with many other counties, Derby also ran the Derby Fighter Plane Appeal. This generated enough money over the years to enable a Spitfire to be purchased by the city, to be named 'The Derby Ram'. Nottinghamshire also contributed to a 'named' aircraft when the town of Retford raised £5,345. With the launching of the fund in September 1940, this amount was achieved by January of the next year. The Spitfire, named 'Retford and District', was delivered from the maintenance unit on 21st March and went to No 611 Squadron based at Hornchurch in Essex. On 6th July it was transferred to No 145 Squadron at Merston in Sussex but was shot down two days later on a patrol over Lille in France. Sadly, the pilot, a Czech named Machacek, lost his life in the crash.

With the Battle of Britain being fought in the skies above the south east corner of the country, the first bomb to drop in the Nottingham area was over the night of 19th August. Four incendiaries fell near Adley Head Farm on the Clumber Estate at approximately 01.05 am. They only caused a little damage but the noise gave civilians the first taste of war. The first air-raid was during the night of 30th/31st August 1940. The thirtieth dawned fair with any early mist soon evaporating as the sun rose. In the south, heavy attacks had been carried out on the south east airfields. As dusk fell, raiders were still coming in, these adventuring far further up country than they had done before. By 10.30 pm, a continuous flow of bombers headed for the Midlands. Though Liverpool was the main target, on the way up country eighteen HE bombs and 120 incendiaries were dropped on Sherwood, mainly around the Mapperley Street and Private Road area, where a bakehouse was set on fire. Whilst much devastation was caused, sadly, a baby became Nottingham's first victim of an air-raid. In addition eighteen people were injured, two very seriously. Two days later, two bombs were dropped on Carlton. The Nottingham blitz had begun.

By the time the Battle of Britain was deemed to have ended in victory for the RAF, the Luftwaffe were sending over reconnaissance aircraft to such potential targets as Rolls-Royce in Derby. The first incident appears to have taken place during the day of 25th October 1940, when a lone Me110 flew over the factory only to be shot down on its way home by Plt Off Norfolk of No 72 Squadron. It crashed into the North Sea just off Yarmouth with the loss of Gefr Gneist, whilst Lt Wacker was picked up by HMS Widgeon and put ashore at Harwich. Incidents like this were chronicled in the ARP diaries, which

Rosenhill Street in Derby devastated by the 15th January 1941 raid.
(Derby Evening Telegraph)

usually gave an account in the most 'laid back' fashion. The dropping of bombs over the night of 19/20th August 1940 are such a case:

"BOMBS DROPPED 19TH/20TH AUGUST 40.
Shaftesbury Crescent – 1 HE.
Corner of Bloomfield St and Reginald Road Schools – 2 HE.
Regent St and Whitchurch St – 3 HE.
88 Canal St and London Rd – 11 HE.
Station Rd – 11 HE.
Bentley St – 4 HE.
Sewage Disposal Land – Holm Lane Spondon – 2 HE. There were further unexploded bombs."

Further incendiaries were dropped on the municipal golf course and the Rolls-Royce testing bed area. The night of 28/29th August saw bombs dropped east of the railway bridge on the Mansfield Road, Stores Road and the racecourse. All were high explosive bombs causing maximum damage. Most of the other attacks on Derby are included in the chapter entitled 'They called it Daimler' but suffice to say that the city had 148 air-raid alerts, the majority of them being false alarms. The final casualty list for Derby was 74 killed, with numerous injuries to others.

Throughout the rest of October and November, there were three more attacks over Nottinghamshire including one daylight raid in the area when five bombs were dropped in Chillwell Lane, Bramcote. No serious injuries were reported. Although the air-raid sirens had sounded in all of these raids, the longest alert for Nottingham was over the night of 28th/29th November, when it lasted from 06.55 pm until 4 am. At the end of a long sleepless night and constant rushing to the shelters, many had to get up next morning and go to work. That year, the people had to make the best they could for Christmas. Despite everything, homes were decorated and although the rationing severely restricted the usual Christmas fare, in the country you could always bag a rabbit or pheasant. The new year began badly when, on 15th January 1941, bombs were dropped on the Colwick Road area. The Wednesday night began quiet but just before midnight, raiders were roaming all over the Midlands. The most serious raids were on the West Midlands but Nottingham and Derby did come under attack. The bombs that fell on the Colwick Road killed fifteen people and seriously injured another fourteen. The next three months saw sporadic raids on the counties, luckily with little loss of life. May 1941, however, was to bring death and destruction to Nottingham on a far larger scale.

With sunset at 9.30 pm and a full moon a few hours later, Thursday 8th May had been a typical spring day. Over the UK, broken cloud had dispersed during the evening to leave moderate or good visibility. Across the English Channel, in the late morning, Luftflotte 3, with its headquarters in Paris and commanded by Generalfeldmarschall Hugo Sperrle, was planning the night's operations. The German High Command had allocated 389 long range and light bombers and 27 long range nightfighters for the raids. All day German groundcrews had been preparing the aircraft, both He111s and Ju17s, for one of the biggest operations of the period. By midnight, these aircraft were lifting off from various airfields in France to begin their night of destruction.

In Nottingham, Thursday night began quietly enough. With the clear, moonlit sky – many called it a 'bombers' moon' – some felt uneasy about what the early hours might bring. As it turned midnight, the sirens began to wail around the city and many people, just about to get into their beds, went instead to their shelters. Down at the Co-Operative Bakery in Meadow Lane, the night shift were baking bread for the next day. Outside, the firewatchers, who were employees of the bakery, and the local Home Guard unit had just finished making tea when the sirens sounded. In the absence of any really heavy raids on the city so far, they again thought that either this was a false alarm or a rogue enemy aircraft had been detected somewhere in the Midlands. Unbeknown to them, 95 aircraft from Luftflotte 3 were approaching the East Midlands intent on bringing death and destruction.

Just outside the city, at Cropwell Butler, a Starfish decoy site had been lit. The large area of waste land was soon ablaze as the oil fired system got underway. Above the crackle and roar of the fire, enemy aircraft could be heard approaching. In actual fact, this Starfish site was intended to fool the enemy into mistaking it for Derby, as Cropwell Butler was the same distance from Nottingham as Nottingham was from Derby. This, plus the fact that interference with the enemy's electronic navigational beams by No 80 Group induced them to drop the majority of their bombs in the Vale of Belvoir, thus saved Derby and Rolls-Royce from a more devastating attack. Nottingham, however, had no such luck as between 00.30 am and 02.38 am, Luftflotte 3 unloaded their bombs on the city: 137 tons of HE and 6,804lbs of incendiaries were dropped, with the main aiming point being an arms factory immediately to the north east of the railway workshops. As the bombers roared overhead, destruction extended from Mapperley Park to the Trentside districts. At 01.00 am, several large explosions indicated that the gas works had been hit, adding to the flames and smoke already ascending from the city. In the centre, bombs had fallen in Shakespere Street, destroying much of Nottingham's ancient University, the Poor Law Offices, Armitage Stores, Moot Hall and Friar Lane. The railway station received a direct hit that destroyed 26 coaches and damaged a further 70.

It was, however, possibly the last three bombs dropped that caused the most loss of life in one spot. The precise moment of impact is faithfully recorded on a clock that stopped at 2 am. The clock at the time was hanging on the wall of the Co-Operative Bakery in Meadow Lane. Two HE bombs struck the bread bakery

Bomb damage at University College, Nottingham city, in 1941.
(Notts Library)

The store of H. Wilkinson in Friar Lane received a direct hit in the 1941 bomb attack. (Notts Library)

whilst one hit the confectionery dept. When the sirens sounded, twenty-two of the staff chose to stay at their posts whilst the rest went down to the basement which was used as an air-raid shelter. As the bombs struck, fourteen out of the twenty-two on the bakery floor survived but nearly everyone in the shelter perished as the building caved in. The explosions had caused the upper building to collapse, rupturing the water mains and further allowing water from the nearby River Trent to flow in. Of the shelter below, both entrances were blocked with debris as well as machinery. Flour had poured everywhere quenching some of the flames, though not enough to allow people to survive. Two men somehow managed to crawl out whilst the other forty-eight men and one woman perished. When next morning the day shift arrived, they found no factory, no bread nor flour. For the next month or so supplies were brought in from several Midland towns, ensuring that bread was once again on the menu.

The shelter beneath the bakery was not the only one to have harboured death. When the bombs began to fall, many people rushed to the shelter in Daykene Street. It took only one bomb to kill twenty-one men, women and children when it penetrated the factory above. Tons of rubble and, again, machinery poured down on the helpless people who had taken refuge in what they knew to be a specially strengthened shelter. One young man who helped in the rescue recalled what he had seen to the local newspapers:

"When the bomb came down, the factory floors collapsed and the heavy engineering machinery came through. We went down to the shelter. There was rubble everywhere. The pillars supporting the arches had collapsed but you could see through the tops of the archways that had crashed down to the floor and see the bunks with legs and feet sticking out through the rubble.

"There were quite a few people injured but all those who were trapped were dead, crushed or smothered. There were a group of demolition workers all scrambling around. I found two people, a mother and her baby, in there. The baby was underneath the mother. Both dead. Smothered. It made me cry, it was so horrible."

The emergency services, ARP and Civil Defence rushed to the aid of the dying and injured. In many cases they found only limbs. The rest had perished in either the explosions or the ensuing fire. Pieces of shrapnel had caused most of the injuries, some of which were attended too in the ambulance, although the majority of victims had to be hospitalised. All the local undertakers were summoned to the scene and the Victoria Swimming Baths were used as a mortuary.

The morning of 9th May dawned and only then could the full extent of the horror and damage be seen. Apart from the Co-op Bakery, the Lace Market had suffered very badly, as had Boots' factories in Poplar Street, Island Street and Station Street. Except for the outer walls, the pillars and arches, St Christopher's Church in Colwick Road was entirely destroyed. The same bomb also annihilated the adjoining Church Hall and Institute. St John's Church in Leenside was also completely gutted. The wooden pews helped fuel the fire that took hold, ensuring that it burned for many hours. Damage was done to the roof of the South Transept of St Mary's Church and many incendiaries fell into the graveyard. Outside the city, several other areas had suffered badly. The West Bridgeford area had received sixty-two HE bombs, with Beeston and Stapleford being hit by twenty-eight HE bombs. In Bingham Rural District, ninety-two bombs fell and incendiaries were dropped on Langar-cum-Barstone and Granby-cum-Sutton. Taking the entire area, four hundred and twenty-four HE bombs had fallen that night destroying two hundred houses and making another two hundred and fifty unfit for habitation. A further two hundred houses were badly damaged and four thousand slightly damaged. Over that one night, two hundred and nine incidents were reported with in excess of one hundred and fifty killed. Nearby at West Bridgeford, another forty were killed with several more at Beeston. Luftflotte 3 had done their job well and it was a night that Nottingham people would never forget.

Not that the *Nottingham Evening Post* of Friday 9th May 1941 would let them. The headlines, incorrectly, ran: 'Sharp raid on E Midlands town – incendiary and HE bombs dropped over a wide area – considerable damage done – casualties not unduly heavy'. It followed with: 'For some time raiders and fighters played a game of hide and seek and there was a spectacular period during which the sky was illuminated with the flash of guns coupled with the roar of anti-aircraft shells bursting. Tracer bullets, the crackling of machine-guns from the fighters, the long fingers of searchlights stabbing and sweeping the sky and vapour trails made by the fighters as they swept around in the brilliant moonlight.'

The next night, with the work of clearing the rubble and listening for signs of life continuing, the enemy returned. As the red hot embers of the buildings were being dampened down by the firemen, death came once again to the city. A lone Ju88 of Kampfgeschwader 76 operating from Creil in France attacked an ordnance factory. Coming down to 300 feet, it dropped HE and incendiary bombs, not all of them hitting the target. As it swooped low over Wilford and Queen's Drive, one hit a house, killing a mother and her daughter. As the flames began quickly to spread, the Fire Service arrived but it was too late to save any of the house, by then a blazing inferno. Local reports stated that the aircraft then returned and machine-gunned the firemen and the civilians in the street.

The last major attack on the city was on the 14th, this time a day raid. Bombs were dropped on Canal Street causing several injuries but no deaths. After this a more peaceful period followed, allowing the clearance of buildings and the funerals of

One that did not return – a Ju88 is guarded by army personnel. (MAP)

the dead to go ahead. The Co-Operative headed the burials by placing a memorial to the dead in the Wilford Hill Cemetery at West Bridgeford. This marked the site of a mass grave for people who could not positively be identified. The Co-Operative also arranged for individually inscribed headstones to be placed at the same location, bearing the names of those who could be identified. The day of the funerals was harrowing for all concerned. Many expected that another raid would develop just as they were saying farewell to their loved ones. But on this cold, melancholy day, the relatives were spared any interruption and the dead were laid to rest peacefully.

Over this sad period, Nottingham had received nearly 90% of all its wartime bombs. Mention must be made once again of the Nottingham War Savings Campaign. By 12th August 1944, this had made £38,237, a considerable sum. Some of the money was to help the people of the county who had suffered at the hands of the enemy. In 1966, those killed at the bakery were again remembered when a commemorative plaque was unveiled at the Co-Operative Wholesale Society's bakery in Meadow Lane by Mr. C T Forsyth, former Managing Secretary of the Nottingham Co-Operative Society. A dedication service followed conducted by the Rev F G Hoye of St Saviour's Parish Church. Many amongst the congregation were survivors from that dreadful

The memorial plaque to those who lost their lives at the Co-op Bakery on 9th May 1941. (Notts Archives)

night, each with his or her own memory of Nottingham's darkest hour.

Although subject to the odd raider, no further large scale attacks were carried out. On 24th July 1942, a lone raider dropped bombs on Sneiton Dale District, killing a firewatcher. Nottingham and Derby, although cultural cities, were not singled out for one of the enemy's 'Baedeker' raids. These were planned raids on cities such as Canterbury, Coventry and Norwich, which had been chosen from the cultural maps drawn by Karl Baedeker, a German publisher.

It was not known at that time that very close to Nottingham was a German POW camp. Not until 1946 was an account officially released giving details and allowing a journalist from the *Nottingham Journal* to visit. It was named Norton POW Camp and was tucked away at Cuckney within a mile or so of Welbeck Abbey. Commanded by Major A E Boughton, it had Nissen huts, flower and vegetable plots with the only difference between this and an army camp being a rusty, very high wire fence. Living behind this fence were German prisoners who were captured in

German POWs working on the gate house of Nottingham Castle, c. 1945. (Notts Archives)

the Middle East, mostly on Russian, British and American fronts. They had been sent to Cuckney from other camps in England to train as teachers or pastors, most of them having attained a certain educational and theological status in civilian life. This was the only POW camp in the country to house such people and one that was free from the Nazi doctrine. Many of the prisoners were 'human guinea pigs' when it came to the question of scholars upon which the trainee teachers could practise. There were certainly no violent prisoners here and only one escape was ever attempted. That ended in failure. Most of the men were content to sit the war out knowing that in the end they would

Tuesday, 8th May 1945, time: 4.15 pm. The crowd gathers in the market place at Derby to hear news of the surrender. (Derby Evening Telegraph)

have qualifications with which to start a new life on their return to Germany.

With the coming of summer 1944, the Allies prepared for their greatest trial, the invasion of occupied Europe code-named 'Overlord'. This entailed vast numbers from the British and American armies to be trained in order for the invasion to succeed. During April and May, over 19,000 American soldiers were stationed in the area, many of them at Wollaton Park with others at Tollerton. Men of the 508th Parachute Infantry Regiment found themselves in unfamiliar surroundings as the count-down to D-Day began. Secrecy was of the utmost importance as a cordon was thrown around the camps. By early June, most of them had gone as the hour of the invasion approached and the Allies were at last to get a foothold on the Continent of Europe.

Today, some people look back at those times and refer to them as the 'good old days', some are still grieving. Victory, however, was a time for celebration and a time for the civilians to begin to rebuild their lives. On 12th April 1941, Winston Churchill, then Prime Minister, spoke in a world broadcast of the spirit of the civilians. "I see the damage done by the enemy attacks; but I also see, side by side with the devastation and amid the ruins, quiet, confident, bright and smiling eyes, beaming with a consciousness of being associated with a cause far higher and wider than any human or personal issue. I see the spirit of an unconquerable people."

GLOSSARY OF TERMS

AA – Ack Ack.
AAF – Auxiliary Air Force.
ADGB – Air Defence Great Britain.
AOC – Air Officer Command.
BATF – Beam Approach Training Flight.
CAA – Civil Aviation Authority.
C in C – Command-in-Chief.
CO – Commanding Officer.
C&M – Care and Maitenance.
EFTS – Elementary Flying Training School.
E&RFTS – Elementary and Reserve Flying Training School.
Fg Off – Flying Officer.
Flt Lt – Flight Lieutenant.
Flt Sgt – Flight Sergeant.
FTS – Flying Training School.
Gp Cpt – Group Captain.
HCU – Heavy Conversion Unit.
HGCU – Heavy Glider Conversion Unit.
LAC – Leading Aircraftsman.
MU – Maintenance Unit.
OCU – Operational Conversion Unit.
OTU – Operational Training Unit.
ORB – Operations Record Book.
(P)AFU – (Pilot) Advanced Flying Unit.
Plt Off – Pilot Officer.
RAAF – Royal Australian Air Force.
RCAF – Royal Canadian Air Force.
RFC – Royal Flying Corps.
RLG – Relief Landing Ground.
RNZAF – Royal New Zealand Air Force.
SLG – Satellite Landing Ground.
Sqn Ldr – Squadron Leader.
SSQ – Station Sick Quarters.
SFTS – Service Flying Training School.
TCG – Troop Carrier Group.
USAAF – United States Army Air Force.
W/O – Warrant Officer.
Wg Cdr – Wing Commander.

BIBLIOGRAPHY

The Squadrons of the RAF – James J Halley – Air Britain 1980.
RAF Squadrons – Wg Cdr C G Jefford, MBE, RAF – Airlife 1988.
The Battle of Britain – Then and Now – After the Battle 1980.
The Blitz–Volumes 1,2 and 3 – After the Battle 1987.
Bomber Command Losses, Volume 7, OTUs 1940/47 – W R Chorle Midland Publishing 2002.
Aircraft of the RAF – Owen Thetford – Putnam 1962.
Actions Stations, Volume 2 – Bruce Barrymore Halpenny – Patrick Stephens 1981.
Wellington – Mainstay of Bomber Command – Peter C Cooksley – Patrick Stephens 1987.
Britain's Military Airfields 1939/45 – David J Smith – Patrick Stephens 1989.
The Narrow Margin – Derek Wood and Derek Dempster – Hutchinson 1961.
RAF Winthorpe – W Taylor – Brayford Press Ltd 1984.
Nottingham at War – Clive Hardy – Archive Publications 1986.
The Bombing of Rolls-Royce at Derby in Two World Wars – Rolls–Royce Heritage Trust (Historical Series No 32) 2002.
Squadron Codes 1937/56 – M J F Bowyer and John D R Rawlings – Patrick Stephens 1979.
Strike Hard – Strike Sure – Ralph Barker – Pan Books 1965.
Enemy Coast Ahead – Guy Gibson VC – Pan Books 1955.
The RAF Builds for War – MOD Air Historical Branch – 1997.
Railway Air Services – John Stroud – Ian Allan 1987.
Per Ardua Adastra – Philip Congdon – Airlife 1987.
Derby at War – Clive Hardy and Russ Brown – Quoin Publishing 1989.
207 Squadron – RAF Langar 1942/3 – Barry Goodwin and Raymond Glynne–Owen – Quacks Books 1994.

Royal Air Force Ashbourne – Malcolm L Giddings – Colerne Debden 1984.

The Burnaston Story – Malcolm L Giddings – Colerne Debden 1991.

Dambuster – Susan Ottaway – Leo Cooper 1994.

Aircraft of the Second World War – K G Munson – Ian Allan 1962.

Fields of Deception – Colin Dobinson – Methuen 2000.

Bases of Air Strategy – Robin Higham – Airlife 1998.

The Victory Book – Odhams Press – 1946.

Thames Valley Airfields in the Second World War: Berkshire, Buckinghamshire, & Middlesex, Robin J Brooks, Countryside Books, 2000.

Kent Airfields in the Second World War, Robin J Brooks, Countryside Books, 1998.

ACKNOWLEDGEMENTS

I acknowledge with grateful thanks all the individuals and organisations who have assisted me in the writing of this book. I list them in no particular order.

Richard Haigh, Peter Felix, David Birch and Brian Walker of the Rolls-Royce Heritage Trust; Roger Parish and the staff of the City of Nottingham Library and Local Studies and Museums Service; Derby Central Library; Brian Taylor; Malcolm L Giddings; Andrew Thomas; Mrs E M Kerry; Flt Lt M Hudson Air Historical Branch 2 (RAF); Ministry of Defence; Len Pilkington; Winston Ramsey; After the Battle; Imperial War Museum; Public Records Office; RAF Museum, Hendon; Maidstone Central Library Springfield; Kent Messenger; Bill Chorley; Laing Technology Group Ltd; Derby Evening Telegraph; Derbyshire Times; 504 Squadron Association; British Parachute Schools; Dept of the Air Force, Maxwell Air Force Base, Alabama USA; David Leatherland of Truman Aviation; Mrs Betty Clements; Mr Tom Stephenson; Wing Leader V Baker, 126 Wing RCAF.

If I have omitted to mention any person or organisation or incorrectly captioned any photographs, please accept my sincere apologies. Final thanks go to my wife as much for her patience as for her proof-reading.

INDEX

Martinet – see *Miles*
Master – see *Miles*
Me109 86–87
Me110 150, 235
Meteor – see *Gloster*
Miles
　Magister 43, 67, 69, 122, 131, 157,
　　195–196
　Marathon 70
　Martinet 43, 63, 81, 82, 126, 152,
　　182, 189
　Master 63, 77, 106, 193
Mosquito – see *de Havilland*
Mustang 100, 185

Napier Lion engines 203
Newton 15, 19, 22, 25, 30, 99,
　115–125, 154, 158, 194
Nottingham Airport 156, 158

Operational Training Units 10 (also
　see 'Other units' index)
Orston 123, 193
Ossington 15, 25, 63, 81, 83,
　126–129, 172
Oxford – see *Airspeed*

Papplewick Moor 19, 101, 130–131
Proctor 63, 188

R.100 Airship 155
R.101 Airship 155
Reserve Flying Training Schools 37
　(also see 'Other units' index)
Retford 85
Roe & Co Ltd, A V 13, 104, 114
Rolls-Royce 13, 25, 56, 75–76,
　90–91, 93–94, 103, 195–201
　passim, 202–219
　Engines:
　　Buzzard 204
　　Condor 203
　　Eagle 203
　　Falcon 203
　　Griffon 93, 209–214 *passim*
　　Hawk 203
　　Merlin 12, 13, 91, 93, 100, 109,

　　168, 199, 202, 206–214 *passim*
　　Meteor 75, 76
　　PV12 206, 208
　　Vulture 12, 174, 210
　　W2B/23 56

S.6 – see *Supermarine*
Sea Lion – see *Supermarine*
Service Flying Training Schools 10,
　37 (see also 'Other units' index)
Short Stirling 10, 50, 59, 141, 144,
　165, 180–185 *passim*
Southern Martlet 156
Spitfire – see *Supermarine*
'Starfish' sites 26
Stirling – see *Short Stirling*
Supermarine
　S.6 204, 205
　Sea Lion 203
　Spitfire 13, 86, 102, 113, 127, 202,
　　208–210 *passim*, 212–214
　　passim
Supermarine-Napier S.5 203
Sutton Bridge 121, 123, 194
Syerston 15, 25, 51, 132–154, 161,
　186, 194

Tiger Moth – see *de Havilland*
Tollerton 15, 121, 155–161, 194
Tomahawk – see *Curtiss Tomahawk*
Tutor – see *Avro*

US Army Engineer Aviation
　Battalions 18

Vampire 3 85, 190
Vickers Wellington 9, 10, 26, 42, 50,
　62, 63, 72–75, 81, 82–83, 85,
　117–119, 126–127, 134, 136, 138,
　144, 152, 171, 172, 176, 189, 191
Vulcan – see *Avro*

Waco
　CG-4A 60
　Hadrian 111
Wallace – see *Westland*
Wapiti – see *Westland*

Squadrons

Other units

Non-British personnel

Czechoslovakian

Polish

Royal Canadian Air Force

US Army Air Force